The TRILOGY Trilogy

The
TRILOGY
Trilogy

ANDREW CALHOUN

Bob,

blessings & laughter,

Andrew Calhoun

Waterbug | CHICAGO, ILLINOIS

ISBN-13: 978-0615701110

Printed in the United States of America

Book design and photo art by Mary Lewis
Cover photo of Andrew by Jenifer Jordan
Back cover photo of Andrew by Danny Schmidt
Proofreading by Ellen Swaim

Thanks to Mary Lewis and early responders Jenifer Jordan and Basho Parks.

Some of these things really happened but not quite in this fashion.
Please don't sue me.

CONTENTS

Trilogy I
The Unbehoven: A Tale of the Old West   1

Part the First Hooves   5
Part the Second On to Hodanga   13
Part the Third The Reckoning   21
Epilogue   29

Trilogy II
Laughter Ours   33

Part 1 Better Bad Puns   37
Part 2 "Because I'm Neurotic"   47
Part 3 Sweating the Big Stuff   51

Trilogy III
The Mem Wars of Andrew Calhoun Trilogy by Andy Goodman   59

Part 1 The Early Years and the Serial Folksinger   63
Part 2 Marriage(s), Children and the Voyage Of Self-Discovery   87
Part 3 Life *Today*   113
Epilogue   121

The
TRILOGY
Trilogy

ANDREW CALHOUN

THE UNBEHOVEN:
A TALE OF THE OLD WEST

ANDREW CALHOUN

THE TRILOGY TRILOGY

I

THE UNBEHOVEN: A TALE OF THE OLD WEST

Unless you can muse in a crowd all day
On the absent face that fixed you;
Unless you can love, as the angels may,
With the breadth of heaven betwixt you;
Unless you can dream that his faith is fast,
Through behoving and unbehoving;
Unless you can die when the dream is past—
Oh, never call it loving.

— ELIZABETH BARRETT BROWNING

THE UNBEHOVEN: A TALE OF THE OLD WEST

PART THE FIRST: HOOVES

If he be of such worth as behooves him, there can not be
a more tedious and unpleasing journey.

— JOHN MILTON

While the horses were all, as one expects, behooved, some were well shod, some unshod, others only shoddily shod. Who would remove the shoes from their shoddily shod hooves? Would new shoes slide into the grooves of the old shoes? Nat hovered about, trying not to get above himself. Suddenly, Nat spoke out! "Tex, shouldn't we re-shoe some of these horses before we head off across the mesa? I mean, look at their hooves!" "It's not a mesa," said Tex. "A mesa is a high flat area.

Not only that, but it behooves us to head West in the morning over this... plain or whatever it is, so we can arrive in town before the Johnson gang." "In that case," responded Nat, "I'll shoe by moonlight." "Great," Tex muttered with muted contempt, "Where are you going to find horseshoes out here?" "I'll find 'em," said Nat, "or die trying." And he walked off across the mesa. They never saw each other again, and the horses, also, went off in different directions. Tex followed the sun for a few days, but always ended up back in the same place. "This could really tend," he said, "to piss me off."

By mid-morning, Nat was approaching the center of the mesa, baking in the hot sun. First he whipped up a few loaves of loofah bread, braided, with poppy seeds; and followed that with some chocolate cupcakes, Kaiser rolls, and a Bundt cake. He caught himself thinking, "how about a Baked Alaska?" and said, "I must be losing it. Of course there's no ice cream out here."

As evening loomed, it occurred to Nat that it would be unwise to fall asleep surrounded by baked goods, which might attract the wild things of the mesa: the coyote, the cougar, the lipitor; the brown bear, and the slightly darker brown bear; so he ate all of the cupcakes, rolls, and the Bundt cake, and, coming upon a small creek, used the loofah bread to lave the crusty trail dirt off his back. Nat trudged on, exhausted. "I thought I'd at least be losing weight out here," he thought, "but then I ate all that stuff." Then, just as he was cresting a small ridge, he was confronted with what was either a brown bear, or a slightly darker brown bear, and, since there was only one, he was unable to discern which sort this was, having no "other" to which to compare it. The slightly less dark (for that is what it was) brown bear began to circle Nat, licking his chops. That is to say, he was licking his own chops, not Nat's. Nat was more than a little terrified; he was trembling, his stomach clenched, the hair stood up on his neck, and he crapped his pants. But to the bear, he didn't look as terrified as he was, only mildly nervous, perhaps, or a little inward. Nat thought of his mother back in Massachusetts, and wondered what she would hear of his death. He thought of the Johnson gang, waiting to have a showdown with him, striding anxiously about. The bear growled.

Nat figured the bear wouldn't go after him until he was done licking his chops. He'd eaten a good number of them, and apparently wanted to lick every last bit of sauce from the bones. This was not the tomato-based sauce known in Texas and most other parts of the nascent nation, but rather the mustard-based variety popular in the Carolinas.

Nat had time to consider his options. He thought of vomiting on himself, and emitting a series of high-pitched shrieks, but he really didn't want to go out that way. Then he thought that maybe he could maneuver over near the gully, and when the bear went for him, grab the bear's head, roll down on his rear, bracing his feet on the bear's gut, and launch it over his head. But there was no gully nearby.

Nat imagined the tick-tick-ticking sound he was hearing was his time running out, as it clicked ever slightly louder. The bear attempted to hypnotize him by staring at him and turning his head to the side, like Crocodile Dundee, but Nat was having none of it. At last the tick-ticking was accompanied by the sound of shuffling feet. Nat turned to look, and the bear, having turned its head to look also, also looked.

Two masked humans sidled inexorably in their direction, lunging and parrying with their foils. As they approached, one said, "Look, it's a bear!" and their arms dropped to their sides, hanging from their shoulder sockets. "What in the world are you doing here?" asked Nat. "We saw a fortune-teller in Omaha who told us it was our destiny to fence in the plains." "Plains??? This is a MESA, you idiots!" cried Nat. "It's not a mesa," said the fencer with yellow tabs on his gloves, "They don't have bears on mesas in this country. And who are you to be calling us idiots, standing in the middle of a mesa with shit in your pants? I ought to suck your eyeballs out of your head." "Well, I didn't ask for the bear to show up here," said Nat.

A green lizard with brown and yellow markings slithered from underneath a rock, darting between Nat and the bear on one side, and the fencers on the other. None of them noticed it particularly, as lizards were dashing about the area all the time anyway. The lizard moved on at about a 42-degree angle to the Northwest, stopped briefly, then disappeared beneath a rock.

"I sure wish there was some ice cream out here," said the bear in a thick Russian accent. "It's hot." "Well," said Nat, "yes, but it's more of a dry heat. What are you doing on a mesa, anyway?" "Look," said the bear, "I was touring with this miserable Russian circus, I escaped in this disguise. Glued into it. Andrew paid me $50 to appear in his novel. Didn't realize I wouldn't be indigenous to the area." Just then a shot rang about from behind an outcropping, killing the bear impersonator— or should I say, the imbearator. A man walked toward them, pistol smoking. The nasty fencer with yellow tabs said, "Aren't you embarrassed? You just shot a bear impersonator." "What a tragedy," thought Nat, "he was only going to appear in this one scene."

Nat's sense of his world was shaken by events. He began to wonder if he really were Nat Brogan, from Massachusetts, or whether he were not, in fact, George Gnesin, scion of a lucrative Philadelphia shipping concern, who had gone into the farm implement business and was headed to San Francisco to negotiate a trade agreement to the Far East.

The fencer with the blue tabs removed her mask and gloves, demanding "Names, boys." Nat said, "George...er... Nat!" and she glared at him dubiously. "I'm Bob," said the man with the gun, "Bob Eucharist." "Eucharist," said the nasty yellow-tabbed fencer, "That's an unusual name. There's not a lot of Eucharists in these parts." "What's yours?" "Andouille Hoover." "Hoover. Mind if I call you Andy?" "Mind if I call you annoying little insect, 'Gnat???' Yes, I mind. Andouille's my name." "Are you named after someone?" "Not that I know of." "How about you?" "Andrea Hoover. But you can call me Andy, Nat." "Okay. Andy and Andouille. It's been a long afternoon. Anybody hungry?"

"Starving," said Bob. "Actually, I was looking forward to eating the bear. You know, save lives, be a big hero, have dinner. Come to find out I shot a guy. You know what they say— 'sometimes you eat the bear, other times you're not allowed to eat the bear because it's a guy glued into a bear costume, and now you're a fugitive.' What have I got to lose now? Let's just eat the damn thing."

Nat began to wish he were somewhere, someone, anywhere but stuck on this mesa with these dastardly individuals. But he was neither as naive nor as dull as he appeared; it occurred to him that he could use these folks' innate viciousness against the Johnson gang, perhaps leading to a bloody free-for-all pitched battle in which all but he and the woman, Andy, would be exterminated.

"Look," said Nat, we're not going to eat the bear." "Of course we're going to eat the bear," Bob shot back (verbally, not with his gun; he shot back in the figurative sense), "Look, we show respect to the bear by using all parts of its body; we eat the meat, use the skin for a coat, make beads out of the teeth, and use the testicles for marbles. This is how we honor the bear. Got it, Brogan?"

Tex, meanwhile, had continued to follow the sun, retracing his steps daily. But as the days passed, the horizon shifted ever so slightly; and at last he found himself approaching the door of a small but well-kept house, and rapped at the door. A woman answered, a broom in one hand and a knotted kerchief around her head. "The name's Tex Tiles, ma'am." "What are you selling?"

"Ain't selling nothing, ma'am," pleaded Tex, "it's just, I been walking back and forth across this— what do you call this area anyway?— for nigh on three weeks without a bath or a decent meal, and I'd be much obliged if you could show me a little bit of Western hospitality." She closed the door, momentarily, in his face, and when she reopened it, Tex found himself staring down the barrel of a 12-gauge shotgun. "I got your 'Western hos'tality' right here." "That's a beautiful gun," said Tex. "I used to have one just like it." "There's no gun just like it," she said, "it was hand-tooled. Anyway, if you want to spend the night here, you'll have to muck out the pig pen." "How do I know you won't just shoot me after I muck it out?" asked Tex. Reflecting a moment, she said, "You're not as dumb as you look. Maybe you could take over the accounting work." "I'd be obliged, ma'am, if you'd let me muck out the pigpen AND take over the accounting work," said Tex, shuffling. And so Tex Tiles became a partner in TASTE, the first Western stand to serve both Texas and Carolina barbecue. He settled down with Rosie, though on busy days he often wished he'd been shot and served to the pigs. Because there is just no accounting for TASTE.

Meantime, on down the mesa, Nat, Andouille, and Andy had sat down for a game of cards. Andy proved to be quite adept with the deck, dealing deftly from top and bottom. "Good thing it's only Crazy Eights," thought Nat. Bob had begun cleaning and gutting the "bear." "Quit that and join us," said Andy, as Bob cast a jaundiced eye over the group. "Throw the other one," said Andouille, "and you'll regret it." Bob took the challenge and flung the other jaundiced eyeball directly at Andouille, bouncing it off his forehead. The men stared at each other. As the tension built, they heard a drumming sound. "If you put that drumming sound with the tap-tapping sound of the foils," thought Andy, "you could do an interesting 3-3-2 against 2-3-3 pattern." A second "bear" approached, running on its hooves. Bob looked round as the bear came clopping up behind him. "Yeah, right, dude. Nice touch with the hooves. Who the hell are you?" The bear stepped forward and dispatched Eucharist to Hades with a couple slaps of her great paws, dragging the corpse off to be eaten. The hooves, glued to her feet by the circus, fell off at last in a river crossing, as the bear headed North to freedom.

They returned to their card game, with Andy playing out

Eucharist's hand. Nat had to ask himself why he found Andy so compelling; her reedy, yet melodious voice; her assured style with dealing the deck. Her neatly tied indigo bandana embracing the lush, dark tresses flowing out and down her back. The way her deft feet would pick up a dropped card or stray pebble— all these things suggesting an emotional depth, a modest yet stubborn integrity and resilient resourcefulness. Also, with the exception of the bandana, she had removed all of her clothing.

THE UNBEHOVEN:
A TALE OF THE OLD WEST

PART THE SECOND: ON TO HODANGA

*There is so much good in the worst of us, and so much bad
in the best of us, it doesn't behoove any of us to speak evil
of the rest of us.*

— EDGAR CAYCE

Nat, Andy and Andouille finished their hand of Crazy Eights. Andy won again. Nat: "Guess we better be gittin' own to Hodanga to take own the Jownson gang. Heard about those guys?" "Oh Andouille," said Andy, "Let's stay right here. We could put down roots right here on this rock! I'd love to become a mesan." Nat, disappointed in his hopes, walked off to furtively shake the turd out of his trousers.

"Honey," said Andouille, "I think we need to get off this gol-durned rock and git along to Hodanga. I'm itchin' to take on Kid Baby & the Johnson Gang. Besides, I need to introduce my library organization concept into some population centers; there's just no way a bunch of lizards are going to spread the news of the Andouille Decimal System." "Lord," said Andy, "this is like a bad novel." "Well it IS a bad novel," said Nat. But that's not our fault. Maybe if we take down the Johnson Gang, Andouille can spread his decimal system far and wide throughout the West." "Yeah?" sneered Andouille, grabbing his crotch, "I gotcha decimal system right here." "Andouille!" cautioned Andy. "We don't know Nat that well." And they walked west, onto the high plains, toward Hodanga.

As afternoon wore on into evening, there were 12,279 lizards that darted across their paths, not that any of them were counting, or would have cared, but that's how many there were. Just a whole lot of lizards. They straggled into Hodanga at nightfall, checking in to Grant's saloon/hotel/brothel, eager for dinner, baths and a good night's sleep. Except Andouille, who threw back whiskies until closing.

Andy and Nat wandered down for breakfast early in the morning, from where they could hear Andouille snoring like a hippo from an upstairs window. Nat had shaven and was hoping Andy would notice how clean he was. Instead she yelled at the waiter, who came over and sat down with them to take their order. He had just come down from Portland, Oregon, and didn't know any better. "No fence meant, ma'am," said the waiter. "It's just that we do things a little different up where I come from. We don't just take your order. We sit down and discuss the entire process of food production with you. Anyhow, it's eggs, beans and toast here, or you could do eggs-eggs-beans, or toast-beans-beans, whatever. Whatever, ma'am. Just don't yell at me. Dudes are sensitive." "I'm not giving you my order until you stand up," said Andy. "Well then I guess a four-cornered relationship is out of the question," said the waiter. "I'll have eggs, beans and toast, pronto," said Nat, trying to defuse the situation. "Who you callin' Pronto?" said the waiter, who really had his back up now. "The name is Andy." "Andy? That's her name, as well. Do you mind if we call you Andrew?" The waiter decided to be a big person, put his ego aside, and get the food order. The customer is always right, even if they're a manipulative, emotionally sadistic drama freak. So he stood up and said, "your order, ma'am?" "Eggs, beans and toast," said Andy, with a Cheshire-cat grin. "Thanks, Andy." Andy put Nat and Andy's order in, walked out the door and headed back to Timber country.

The owner/madam/cook came out with their breakfasts. "Son," she said to Nat, "you look like a fine fella. If you're plannin' to stay in town a spell, I could use a little help around here. Need someone to wait tables, wash dishes, feed the chickens, do laundry. Interested?" "Sure's hell," said Nat. When do I start? "Right soon's you're done. Last two waiters name Andy. Mind if I call you Andy?" "Please just call me Nat," said Nat, and so he came to be known as Matt around the place. His thought was to earn enough money for a gun and a few rounds, and take some gunslinger lessons. One day as he was washing dishes, he began to ask Mrs. Duncan about the Johnson gang. "Heck, she said," I'll GIVE you a gun if you take out those guys. Them guys are bad. Real bad."

So Mrs. Duncan began teaching Nat the ways of the gunslinger, early in the mornings, out behind Grant's. She told him, "Never look at his eyes. Watch his hand. But make sure he's looking at your eyes, and not your hand." "How can I make sure he's looking at my eyes," queried Nat, "if I'm looking at his hands?" Mrs. Duncan laughed and slapped Nat on the butt for the fiftieth time. "What you do is, Matt, when you catch him watching your hands, you reach over and scratch your nuts. He'll be looking at that. Then he'll be surprised enough to look you in the eye. Then you shoot him. That's the only way you can outdraw Kid Baby." "Still," said Nat, "if he's looking me in the eye, I'm not looking at his hands." "Don't argue with me," said Mrs. Duncan, "or I'll shoot you myself."

Andouille and Andy, who had stayed on a few days at the hotel, were discussing whether or not to head west, where they had ambitions of starting an eiderdown farm. Andy was pressing to leave, but Andouille wanted to stay a few more days in order to watch Nat get shot. "Well, what if he beats Kid Baby, Andouille? Gonna challenge him yourself?" "Mebbe," said Andouille. "Mebbe."

Seems everyone in Hodanga— and the surrounding towns of Huizenga and Hodenga— had heard of the upcoming showdown between Matt Brogan and Kid Baby. It was the first gunfight since Kid Baby had gunned down Kid Pedophile the previous August. He'd proceeded to drag him around the town behind a buggy and leave him for the buzzards. Nobody gave Matt much of a chance.

"So why do they call him 'Kid Baby, Mrs. Duncan?'" asked Nat one morning. "Well, he's incompetent, is why, Matt."

"Incompetent?" "Yep. Gots to wear diapers. It's his trademark. I reckons it's one the thing make him so fierce." This odd attribute made him loom all the more terrifying in Nat's mind. Baby seemed to be totally out of control. "But don't you worry," said Mrs. D., "we got a stragedy." Of course, Mrs. Duncan was pulling Nat's leg. But in his fearful condition, he was ready to believe anything. He was improving on his draw, and had managed to shoot a couple of rabbits out back; she found him useful, and liked his company; and she had a plan to hide behind a bush and shoot Kid Baby herself. Unfortunately, the deacon, Mr. Widdington, had removed the bush onto church grounds.

Something rarely seen in that part of the Southwest, appeared— a huge black thunderhead, bringing torrential rains. Everyone forgot about the upcoming gunfight between Brogan and Baby, and watched the weather. New streams appeared. The old, quiet crick that ran out back in three seasons became swollen with pus, spreading recklessly over the countryside. The downpour went on for days. Eventually, the sun returned and, slowly, inexorably, the rivulets dried up and the swollen river became flaccid once more. That is when that little creek got its name— swollen or not, they call it Lake Pus. Nat & Mrs. Duncan resumed their gunslinger classes. "I really ought to be charging you for these lessons," said Mrs. Duncan. "Maybe you could put in a few extra unpaid hours."

Early one morning, as the sun began its slow, inexorable, ascent, Nat stirred briefly on his cot, thought about waking up, then decided to sleep some more. He went into a heavy sleep, and had dreams revealing to him the secrets of his destiny and the keys to his survival, but unfortunately, he didn't remember them when he woke up and slowly, inexorably, yawned. He thought, apathetically, about the upcoming gunfight. "Hound give Huck about it," he muttered aloud. "Kid Baby. Kid Armageddon. Kid Kidd, Kid Bugeyes, Billy the Kid. Billy the Adult. Grandpa the Kid. The Argonaut Kid. Line 'em up. Hound give Huck. Kill 'em all." As he rose to go to the outhouse, he stubbed his toe against the, what do you call that sort of piece of furniture?

Nat was sitting, straining, as was his wont, at his morning bowel movement, when he remembered— a credenza! And he nearly shouted the word— "Credenza!" "A WHAT??" asked a familiar voice from just outside the door. Nat pretended he either hadn't said anything, or hadn't heard the question. "Why are you saying 'credenza?'" It was Andy, waiting her turn. "Because I stubbed my toe on the credenza in my room," blurted out Nat. "That's not a credenza," said Andy. "It's a small bureau. They don't have credenzas on this side of the mesa. Hey," she said, "Mrs. Duncan hired me to do some advance publicity for the gunfight. Anything special you want on the flyers?" "Yeah. It's Nat Brogan, not Matt Brogan. N-A-T. Okay?" "You got it, Matt."

Nat and Andy traded places, she in the outhouse, he outside. "Andy," he said, "the gunfight is in two days. I'm sure as hell nine pounds to a turnip to die in the street. So I got nothing to lose here. I'd like my line to continue. I'm a twenty-six year old man, and my biological cock is ticking. Will you bear my child?" "But I'm married!" she exclaimed. "I know. But your husband's an asshole." "Well, that may be true," shot back Andy, but I'm carrying HIS child as of about a month ago, so I'm not going to be carrying yours. It's out of the question." "This is a tragedy for me," whined Nat. "I was hoping you could carry my seed to spawn, ensuring the Brogan line for posterity. ...Well, how about a blow job, then?"

Eventually he wearied of waiting for Andy to emerge.

Nat wandered out to an outcropping behind an outbuilding, and began to reflect on his life. He thought he'd take a few hours off, with the gunfight coming up in a very few days, to think about the meaning of it all. He was thinking of this as a searching in the wilderness sort of an interlude, but he quickly got bored, and began to practice his spitting. Nobody wants to get shot with drool on their best shirt.

Andouille Hoover stormed into the kitchen where Mrs. Duncan was frying eggs and bacon and boiling cactus & fatback, her signature dish. "Where the hell's that little sumbitch Nat?! I'm gonna kill 'im." "Why?" "Gittin' fresh with my wife, that's why. I'm gon' kill 'im." "No way, Andouille. He's fightin' Kid Baby in two days." "I don't want Kid Baby kill 'im," raged Andouille, "I wan' kill 'im." "Well," says Mrs. Duncan, "you take on Kid Baby first, I'll put Nat up in round two. We've been advertising this thing for weeks." "Deal," said Andouille. Nat, meanwhile, continued his mystical meditative journey behind the outcropping, visiting with the spirits of the mesa, gittin' ready. Gittin' ready.

Andy was hard at work creating and putting up posters: Mrs. Duncan's Gunfights: Round One: Kid Baby vs. Andouille Hoover; Round Two: The Victor vs. Matt "Gnat" Brogun; followed by gunny sack races, mud wrestling with the prostitutes and the church deacons, a barn dance with "new-timey" music; and the following day, The Johnson Gang. At last, Nat emerged from his prayers and meditations behind the outcropping, and went in to worship the breakfast dishes.

THE UNBEHOVEN: A TALE OF THE OLD WEST

PART THE THIRD: THE RECKONING

It behooves us to accomplish what God requires of us, even when we are in the greatest despair respecting the results.

— JOHN CALVIN

Mrs. Duncan bustled in, flapping her arms like a chicken. "Little gal out there wants talk a chew. I'll finish these up." So Nat wandered into the breakfast area, encountering a statuesque woman of his own age, wearing sensible shoes and her hair pinned back in a severe bun. It was the most obdurate, pitiless bun he'd ever seen. And Nat, being from Massachusetts, knew his buns from a hole in the ground. "Hello?" "Are you Matt

Brogan?" "Well, not exactly, my name is Nat Brogan." "Well is Matt around here, then?" "No, I'm him, you see, people get my name wrong, and call me Matt." "And you let them?" Nat looked sheepishly at his shoes, which he noticed were sorely in need of polish. "What's your name, ma'am?" "I'm not your mam. My name's Ann Dewey. I'm a reporter. I'm doing a human interest piece on this gunfight. Maybe you can tell me how you got into this gun fighting business." "Look," said Nat, "I'm getting gunned down in the street out there in a couple days. I have to do a damn interview on top of it?" "Most gunslingers like publicity," said Ann. "How fascinating. Have you always been publicity shy?" "I'm taciturn. I don't talk to the media," said Nat. "Well I just don't know what I'm going to do if you won't talk to me," said Ann Dewey, pouting. But the pout was constrained by the severity of her bun, which had pulled her eyebrows up on her forehead, so that when she pouted they came back to a normal position. So she looked serene, while trying to appear downcast, thus merely confusing the man she was trying to manipulate. They stared blankly at one another, waiting for something to happen.

Andouille rambled in from the front door, in a rare cheery mood, but when he saw Nat, his visage glowered and darkened like a thunderstorm in the Smoky Mountains, where his grandmother was from, although she had been deceased a few years now and he had never really known her well. "I'm gon' kill you on Sar'dy," he said. "Are you Kid Baby?" asked Ann Dewey. "No, I'm Andouille." "Well, I'm Ann Dewey, Andouille. I see you're up first to fight Kid Baby." "That's just so I'm the one gets to kill this little jerk." This was news to Nat. What if Andouille managed to survive Kid Baby? He'd be squaring off against someone he really didn't like very much. Where was the honor in that? He didn't realize Mrs. Duncan was setting up a sort of three-ring circus, and charging an entrance fee. Nat had been expecting to die in the street, tragically and without fanfare. As it happened, there was going to be a small brass band warming up the crowd for the gunfight; food vendors, including a taco stand and a "create your own peanut butter and jelly sandwich" bar; and a photographer named Papa Rotsy taking photos of people dressed in vintage clothing from the previous century.

Nat didn't understand why Andouille and Ann Dewey were so much better informed than he on the upcoming event; but that's what you get for doing your turn in the wilderness. He was particularly annoyed by the "create your own sandwich" concept. "What's next, a soup stand that puts out a pot of boiling water, raw carrots, potatoes, onions, you have to catch and kill the chicken?"

"Now you're thinkin', Matt!" Watching Andouille being interviewed by Ann Dewey, Nat felt a jealous pang. She let her hair down as they talked, and it flowed mellifluously, if that is a word, over her shoulders. Despite Nat's best efforts to avoid publicity and die in the street like a dog, his dirty laundry would now be known all over the mesa, and Andouille would be seen as a hero defending his wife's honor.

So Nat lurked around in the back of the room, listening to Andouille's life story. He hadn't realized that Hoover had been born and lived in Belgium in his early childhood, going on to matriculate in France, then starting the first California winery in Prussia, prior to becoming a famed hurler touring Highland games. Ann Dewey appeared fascinated, her eyes glistening like well-buttered potatoes. Nat could bear it no longer; and so when the Andouille interview had concluded, he sheepishly approached the table and consented to be interviewed as well. "Well!" exulted Ann Dewey, "I thought you didn't like publicity, Matt!" "Oh yes, that's right," said Nat, and went back on upstairs to take a nap. Ann never did get her interview with Nat.

Nat slept through the night, waking to the song of whatever bird it was that was indigenous to that area at that time; I'd tell you their names, but Nat didn't know them, and we're really, though not going all first person here, telling Nat's story. So, he woke up and headed down to serve breakfasts. "Mrs. Duncan," enquired he, what are you going to do if I'm gunned down? Who's going to serve?" "Oh, don't worry about that, Matt," said Mrs. Duncan, "I'll find some fella or gal to do your job in a heartbeat. I probably shouldn't tell you this, but you're sort of a morose chap— the kinda guy thinks too much. People don't like you. If I weren't grooming you for the showdown, you'd-a been down the road long since. Although I must say, you're really kinda cute," and she slapped his butt. Nat went and stood at the back door, arms akimbo, looking out at the glowing morning, the morning lovely, mysterious, glistening with the hope of new beginnings 'neath a beaming firmament. "Why you gotcha arms all weird like that?" said Mrs. Duncan, "there's a custma jes' come in. "I'm practicin' my Akimbo steps," said Nat, "he'll just have to wait a few seconds."

And so at last, slowly, inexorably, the day arrived, like any other. The saloons were full, the little boys ran about shrieking in piercing, high-pitched voices. Nat thought, "I'm dying today.

Maybe I could just shoot a few of those kids first and get some peace and quiet around here." But he is to be forgiven such thoughts. There was Papa Rotsy, taking and selling his photos. And there in the distance, his magnificent white stallion kicking up a plume of golden dust, hallooing and waving his black and silver hat, was Kid Baby.

They lined up in the street, all of the men with exactly three day's growth, the women displaying their cleavage and profound, virtually Buddhist concern, the children no longer shrieking in that annoying way, especially the little boys, no longer running in circles and just screaming and screaming until it feels like the top of your skull is going to fly off and you wish they were muzzled like horses; and Kid Baby rode in.

He was chewing on a bullet. "Who's first?" he asked. "I am," said Andouille. And they stood in the street, squinting at each other with their hips swaying back and forth, their hands positioned over their guns. Then Andouille started laughing, threw off his gun belt and stood there, reeling about with his arms spread wide. "This is ridiculous!" He shouted. "I have nothing against this man! Let us all just live together in peace!" Kid Baby shot him, thus ending the possibility of introduction of the Andouille Decimal System to the nation's library system. A rather inefficient quarter century later, Melvil Dewey would develop and introduce a similar program.

Nat waited until the coroner had dragged Andouille's blood-spattered, dusty corpse off the street. Andy was being interviewed by Ann Dewey. "This is a real tragedy for you, isn't it Andy? A real tragedy?" "Yup," said Andy. "Definitely. Not what Andouille and I had in mind when we came out to fence in the mesa." "I'm sorry for your loss," said Dewey, demonstrating, despite her professional role, a great deal of compassion for her fellow woman. Papa Rotsy sidled in to get some shots of the keening Andy weeping over the corpse.

"Who's next?" said Kid Baby.

"I am," said Nat. "You Matt Brogan?" "Nope. It's Nat Brogan." "I thought I was taking on Matt Brogan. I didn't ride all the way out here to take on no 'Nat Brogan'. Matt Brogan's the guy what done kilt my pa." "Look, my name's Nat Brogan. Matt Brogan's a different guy. No relation. I've heard of him though. He's an importer of Kilts and Sporrans. He's kilted lots of guys." "Well okay. I'll kill you jest as good," said the Kid.

Kid Baby and Nat stood in the street, squinting at each other, their hips swaying back and forth, hands hovering over guns. It wasn't really necessary for Nat to be squinting, because the sun was behind him; but he figured that was how it was done. Kid Baby asked himself— "Why is this dude squinting?" Nat didn't feel much of anything, not even dread. He just stood there, getting ready to shoot, staring at the other man's eyes. It was what it was. A pair of rough-legged hawks circled lazily, high in an otherwise birdless sky. Kid Baby kept swaying his hips, back and forth, then round and round, and Nat began to mirror him, squinting, swaying, staring. A leopard-banded gecko popped out from underneath a sullen, sunken wheelbarrow with wood as gray as stone: slowly, inexorably, it made its way through the suddenly windless dust until it stood between the two men, scratching at a small stone. Then all at once it darted and fled— a fleeting thought— into the rut on the opposite side. Nat and Kid Baby continued to stare, to assess, to sway, back and forth, round and round, with the hips, hands hovering and unbehovering over their guns. Nat thought to himself the last thing he'd expected to think, something he had never thought before, exactly what he was reading in the other man's face: "I want to fuck this guy." And standing, swaying, squinting, they made a deal with their eyes. Kid Baby shot first, and Nat heard the bullet whistle by his left ear. Nat Brogan shot, just over the top of Kid Baby's head, aiming for the top of his hat. He missed, and the bullet went directly into Kid Baby's brain. The notorious outlaw lurched forward, folded, flopped, and settled in the dust, as dead as a doornail. "Shit!" said Nat.

Nat was mobbed. Mrs. Duncan fell on top of him, breaking his arm above the elbow. Boys circled, shrieking once again. Papa Rotsy oozed through the crowd and was working his way in for a close-up, when Nat performed a sit-out and clocked him with his good arm. Ann Dewey winked at him. But her bun was still so tight that she wasn't able to fully wink, and it merely looked like a narrowing, a narrowing of the eyes. She was inviting him for a night of passionate lovemaking, but the message conveyed was one of vague disapproval. Nat was lifted up by strong arms and carried into the saloon, his useless right arm throbbing, and plied with whiskey and beer and rum and cognac and brandy and vodka and tequila. Mrs. Duncan set his arm and bound it up in a sling. Then she poured brandy on it and lit it on fire, laughing and whooping like a banshee. The bartender threw a bucket of water over the both of them.

The coroner's report revealed an odd fact: Kid Baby was hiding a physical abnormality in his tooled and burnished cowboy boots; rather than the expected feet, he had hooves at the end of each leg. And so the mystery was explained: Kid Baby never really had a choice about it; he was behooved by fate to be a badman, a gunslinger in the West.

There ain't much more to tell, except that the Johnson Gang turned out to be just a ragtag bunch of guys who played fiddle, banjo, guitar and washtub bass. They came through town that night, and, despite his bad right arm, Nat was able to take them out one at a time with his left hand pumping the pistol, as they stepped forward in turn to take their breaks on "Mama Don't Allow." He felt bad about it after he sobered up.

Nat headed back to Massachusetts, became a turnip farmer, and is lost to history. The farmer's job is to produce produce, and I reckon he did that. And so we make our farewell to Nat Brogan, a man who faced the ultimate challenge: who did as he did not because he chose to, but because it was required of him by destiny; because he felt, in his heart of hearts, that he was so behooved.

THE UNBEHOVEN: A TALE OF THE OLD WEST

EPILOGUE

And I indeed will show my high descent to the city, striking home to my heart with the sword; but thee, on the other hand, it behooveth to act in concert with my bold attempts.

— EURIPIDES

All of the characters in this story, the good and the bad; the actual historical characters such as Bob Eucharist and Mrs. Duncan, and the fictional creations, such as Ann Dewey and Tex Tiles, having demonstrated varying appropriate degrees of behoovefulness, are dead now. They have gone on. And so, as the deer-skin covered wagon of our Western tale hoves to, the essential question remains for all of us— for each of us— for me and for you: Are we, truly, the behoven?— or, like Nat Brogan: The *Unbehoven?*

Andrew Calhoun

LAUGHTER OURS

BOOK OF THE YEAR

· PROPHYLACTIC HUMOR SERIES ·

C H

CONDOM
HOUSE

THE TRILOGY TRILOGY

II
LAUGHTER OURS

*The discovery of this Behooving Machine was
the discovery of the political perpetual motion.*

— CHARLES DICKENS

LAUGHTER OURS
PART 1: BETTER BAD PUNS

Hale forth the Carroch— trumpets, ho,
A flourish! run it in the ancient grooves—
Back from the bell! Hammer! that whom behooves
May hear the League is up!

— ROBERT BROWNING

George Washington demanded to be taken down from Mt. Rushmore. Said he was tired of being taken for granite.

My friend from Georgia got frustrated he couldn't make himself understood at the Chicago area drive-throughs. The problem was that he was going through with drawl.

He had a pronounced drawl, which he pronounced "drawl."

My friends have disappeared into the fog. They will be mist.

I'm trying to master the Midwestern twang, but finding it impassable.

An explosive form of slang dialect is developing in the upper Midwest. It's called the vernucular.

When in-laws are outlawed, only outlaws will be in-laws.

My uncle's a pervert. But that's natural when you have vernuncular degeneration.

Visitors coming from Milwaukee. Prepare for the wurst.

The expression "to get all gussied up" comes from Akron, Ohio, which makes it an Akronism.

It was 105 degrees at the Hoover Dam, and the tour guide was doggedly extolling its attributes when he collapsed in the heat, fainting with dam praise.

Schindler Elevator Corporation is taking escalators to the next level.

We're rehearsing the Louis Prima tribute show. Is it too early to begin plans for a Prima tour?

I received an offer from the New Life Ministry. They said I was preordained.

Agnostics are on the awe fence.

When life gives you lemons, vote.

How many roads must a man walk down before you call him a taxi?

Washington is broken. It needs a new ballcock valve.

Heard a psychologist on a talk show say that it's important to men's self-esteem to receive oral sex. I guess she was saying we need phallidation.

When pigs fly, they'll be pigeons.

A vegetarian diet is healthier for the planet, but tofu people are practicing it.

If you go to a sauna, well, you know hot ease these days.

Sometimes people feel it's cheaper to send out regrets than to pay for all their friends to attend their nuptials. So they make a nupology.

I entered the grand ballroom, where the celebrants were intertwining and dining, and danced a pod-de-deux with a body snatcher.

"There's no bomb in my bed, honey. That just cotton ticking."

Steve Tate died. They're having an S. Tate sale.

Saturdays I get down and dirty. Sundays I get up and clean.

You never forget how to paint a car. It's like writing a bicycle.

I found an old box of girl scout cookies in mint condition.

If you atrophy enough, you can become a trophy.

Type 2 diabetes is a cancer among today's youth.

Painful hemorrhoids? See an anusthesiologist.

I'm taking my anxiety disorder down the yellow brick road, ostensibly.

I have this rotating fan that keeps tipping itself over. I'm looking for a new fan base.

Last week I went down to US Bank to make a deposit and they had a guy at the door bantering with customers, he was a pretty darn good punster too! The teller told me that due to these competitive times the district manager had told the local branches to put out a bank wit for the customers on Thursdays.

The bank was robbed, and they suspect the heist was an inside job; the dividends manager has been named as a person of interest.

I went to a meth-head acting workshop. Asked a young lady name of Laura out for lunch.

"Well," she said with a sly grin and coke-headish shake of her curls, "maybe on Thursday."

When she lets her hair down, Laura puns a lot. It's the lowest form of human hair.

My calf has been bothering me. Probably misses its mother.

Egrets— I've had a few. But then again...too few to mention

The alleged thief anticipated a knife in the ribs, it being a constabulary.

Yale's quarterback would have called an audible, but figured it would be redundant.

It is time for the players of croquet to lay aside their mallets and turn from their wicket ways.

He said, "check mate." So I gave him the check. He said that's not what I meant. So I went to call my girlfriend.

Fishermen can trawl their own destiny.

The Nike Lunar Glide said to the New Balance Cross Trainer; "We shoe have come a long way. Remember when we were all just Keds?"

A carpet seller in our town has opened a liquor bar for browsers, and renamed the business "Alcohol and Rugs."

The Mayor said that we all need to make sacrifices. Chicagoans, bring your goats and chickens to the Daley Plaza at sunrise on Thursday.

Stopped by the Brookfield Zoo. There was a zebra there that was hung like yak.

An ant, simply exploring its world, crawled onto a sleeping bird's wing. Suddenly the bird awoke and flew high in the sky. The ant was able to burrow in amongst the feathers, and eventually came back to earth, at some distance from home. When it had crawled the long distance home to its hill by late the following morning, the head ant scolded him for not helping out with the hill's expansion project: "We've all been working hard here, while you were just off on a lark."

And so the ant was ostracized. But rather than stick its head in the sand, it created The Declaration of Independants. This antiestablishment manifesto led to the proliferation of independant artists and labels as we know them today. This groundbreaking insect also wrote the self-help book, Codependant No More.

Breakfast? A large omelette, four eggs ample.

I would share my coffee secrets, but I don't want to get into hot water.

A first kiss is a good lipmus test of a relationship.

My belly dancing costume arrived, but I sent it back due to the undue lading charge.

Sometimes when a doorknob handle keeps falling off, it works to turn it around and screw it back in on the other side. This technique is known as reverse knobbery.

Henry is here with the stone, sharpening all the axes and knives. I always cry at whettings.

"Oh, HANG the laundry!" exclaimed Harry. Can't you wait to put it in the dryer until we get home?

Om is where the art is.

Our chamber group leader is improvising with the Pachelbel piece; something of a loose canon. Finally we were sliding so far off pitch that he nearly lost his temper. But he composed himself, and said, "It's in D. Please make a note of it."

The fiddler is composing a jig in the hunky-dorian mode.

Check out the new folk metal band, The Tungsten Trio.

Existential theatre: performin' Sartre.

Things might have gone differently for Othello had he not drunk of Iago's sangria.

Walks and meals are the warp and woof of a dog's life.

I put my dog down yesterday. Said, "Hobo, you've got delusions of adequacy."

There's a terrific new product from Abe foods, a natural anti-coagulant that takes the lumps out of cake, pancake and waffle batter. Ask for Abe Batter-ease.

The new Mr. Potato Head turns the concept of the old Mr. Potato Head on its head.

There are new tureens with a neck for pouring. Would you like a neck tureen?

Since verbs are verbiage, why isn't garb garbage? e.g., "He put on his best garbage and went to the palace."

You can learn more about clothing by watching "Everybody Loves Raiment" on the Home Shopping Network.

Just off the top of my head: a beret.

A man's comb is his hassle.

She was his beard. He was hirsute.

If you can't shave the world, shave yourself instead.

All these hours spent shaving over a hot stove— does anyone appreciate it?

My cousin Ed Goodman was going to U Colorado as a freshman and trying to room with his long-time best friend, Ed Fowler. But the university wouldn't allow co-Ed housing.

Edgar and Edwina had differing reports about what happened in the booth with the bearded lady. It was a he's Ed, she's Ed situation.

I thought about heredity, and his also.

The cost of ear bud replacements has put her in arrears.

The cost of sharpies has gone up markedly.

Since her papers were being held up, she filed for an extension on her thumb tax.

The teacher chalked his asthma problems up to the blackboard.

Remember to give to those in heat this holiday season.

If you're looking to start a car, finding the ignition is key.

After removing a wood tick, always swab the skin with rubbing alcohol. This prevents infection from tick toxicity.

A new mattress? I'll get right on it. I'm inclined to lie down.

If I were a bedding man, I'd lay money on Beautyrest.

Opinions are like diverticulae.

Can 8 billion acidophilus and bifidus be wrong?

What happens if a class has more than one valid dictorian?

Do lobsters masturbate?

Sure, this time the whale was able to flip the boat over. But I think it was a fluke.

Sometimes people with serious illness become persisently voluble and loquacious, wasting their precious energy. It's a toxic combination.

The only thing that would ease his anxiety was to down a half pound of feta cheese. He texted his wife to pick some up on the way home. She wrote back that it was a feta calm plea.

Those who eat oranges can be divided into the halvers and the halve nots.

I attended a sugar retreat. I've always been a sucker for hard candy.

I prefer the aloe path in medicine.

At Walgreens, you can get Wal-tussin, Walitin, Wal-phed. Eventually they'll be selling Walijuana.

I've been waiting on the tarmac for three hours. The chilimac was fantastic, so I figured it'd be worth it.

Coming from First Class, I issued fourth with my luggage.

The jeweler said he could put Mickey Mouse hands on the Rolex. I said, "Not on my watch."

Watch for falling temps here in Chicagoland. They drank after work, and slipped on the ice.

Finally, a white collar job. Shovelling snow.

There seems to be a lot of snow still on the driveway. It doesn't weigh much, but there's a ton of it.

Our neighbors made a scantily clad snow maiden after the blizzard. Today she's wearing a thawing bikini.

Looked for the ice block, but it was gone— solid gone.

We've had a ninja reign since Thursday.

When I worked at the mortuary I was alarmed by the sight of a corpse where the hand had just been cut off, so I went home to journal about it. Morgue wrist for the writer's mill.

Nothing is certain in life but death and Texas.

When I pass, I'd like to be cremated and tossed into the sea, as while I may not be heaven bound, I am fit to be tide.

DEFINING OUR TERMS

Behooveful: Behooveful \Be*hoove"ful\, a. Advantageous; useful; profitable. [Archaic] — Be*hoove"ful*ly, adv. — Be*hoove"ful*ness, n. [Archaic] — Webster's Unabridged Dictionary, 1913 edition.

Hintstincts: genetic predispositions to suggestiveness

Indistincts: genetic predispositions to vagueness

Hindsight: an eyeball staring out of an asshole

Eubonics: dialect spoken by talk show hosts

Conanism— early withdrawal of talk show hosts

Hoosier hosieredundance: Indiana residents wearing socks over nylons

Circumcision: A decision made in a roundabout way

Sardonic: a restorative, omega-3 rich hair tonic made from sardine oil.

Mockudentary: a comedy about Dentists

Despontiff: a depressive Pope

LAUGHTER OURS
PART 2: "BECAUSE I'M NEUROTIC"

Then did they ask a thousand questions of Don Quixote, but he would answer to none of them, and only requested them to give him some meat, and suffer him to sleep, seeing rest was most behooveful for him.

— CERVANTES

I excel at sleeping. I make it look easy.

I dreamed I was sitting on an ottoman, which turned, suddenly, into a divan, then a sofa, then a couch.

Bright, sunshiny morning. Not into it.

Sometimes I wonder if life has cast me as "Piggy" in *Lord of the Flies*.

My lists of things to do have become the new mess.

I only check facebook because I can't face my checkbook.

I'm oppressed by a plethora of ephemera.

I'm all for boding, even if I don't bode well.

I failed a drug test today. Misspelled "cortisone."

I would be VERY surprised if the moon suddenly exploded.

I just found out that I'm a placebo! Maybe that's why I'm not working.

I'm thinking about a terrific salad. If there is such a thing.

If you don't like my horse novels, ride your roan.

I'm a master of my craft. Well, so it's a little plastic one.

I joined the diving club because I wanted to make a splash.

I was a skipper aboard a man-o-war, until they took away my jump rope.

I've had it up to here with the neck problems.

People recommend stretching. But I think stretching is bullshit.

Back from the dentist. My teeth are clean enough to eat off of!

I'm looking forward to a soft twisty ice cream cone dipped in hot magma. I don't imagine it will be edible, but it will be unique, at least until the second one is served.

Invested in a bullshit detector a couple months back, it cost $299.99, but so far I don't think it's working. I thought about returning it but the company is no longer on-line.

They say beauty is only skin deep, but try removing the brains and skull and see what you have left of your beauty.

A wasted day. I spent half of it dulating, and the other half undulating.

I'm having a pique experience.

I swear by my malfunctioning printer.

I'm practicing for a "how to destroy electronic equipment" presentation.

I had to say "infrastructure" thrice within an hour, wore down and went to bed early.

I'm sick and tired of people complaining all the time.

Reasonable people may differ, but not with me.

As a matter of fact, I AM chopped liver. This is a problem?

Sometimes I feel patronized by my customers.

I still believe in common courtesy, thank you very much.

New abbreviation— ISFYL— I'm sorry for your loss.

New alter ego, only for home: Joe Malone. I'm Malone in the house.

I went to the store to get some head cheese. They told me to look in the head case. But the case was closed.

I got lost on my way to the errant water show and wound up at a mental block party.

They say, "He puts his pants on one leg at a time." But what if that's not true; what if he actually sits on the edge of the bed and pulls on both pant legs at once?

You've heard the old saying, "Money can't buy potatoes"? It's not true.

I'm working on a diorama demonstrating the habits and habitats of various grazing animals. But I can't seem to get my yak together.

My sister was great at this kind of thing. She was always such a diorama queen.

Eat healthy, live well, hurl plates and glasses.

There comes a time in a person's life when he must put away childish things, and order a pizza.

For the wise man keeps his counsel. The wise man doesn't just walk into total strangers' homes at 3 in the morning and start throwing shit around.

If your pills are getting wet and you don't have a bottle or plastic bag handy to put them in, use a condom.

I asked my optometrist about these weird marks in my palms. He said it's probably astigmataism.

Candida is the yeast of my worries.

A few days of bloat, but I think I'm kicking gas today.

I've begun selling my goiters, which can be purchased individually, or in bulk for a lump sum.

LAUGHTER OURS
PART 3: SWEATING THE BIG STUFF

Oh, I hear the people calling through the day time and the night time,
They are calling, they are crying for the coming of the right time.
It behooves you, men and women, it behooves you to be heeding,
For there lurks a note of menace underneath their plaintive pleading.

— ELLA WHEELER WILCOX

The universe began with a couple of huge sonic boobs.

The universe just took over the planet. Try to remain calm.

The editors of *Science Today* stated that the vegetarian dinosaurs pre-dated the predators.

I love this planet. It means the world to me.

If you want an Earth Day decal, sticker round.

I've lived through the nuclear terror of the Cold War, worries of Y2K, Global Warming and prophecies of the Mayan Calendar. Armageddon tired of the doomsday scenarios.

Life ain't easy for a boy named Nebuchadnezzar.

We're just back from a whirlwind tour of tornado country.

Even if you're in the hurricane's path, it doesn't mean you can't havoc good day.

They gave the order to evacuate. My uncle Terry said "No problem, I was evacuating anyway."

Labyrinth, repeat. Labyrinth, repeat.

What are trolls made of?— Gnome matter.

The goddess spun in the center of the whirlwind. At last we realized that we were getting a precious opportunity to watch the whirled Ceres.

Back in the day, it was mid-afternoon. And at the end of the day, it's still mid-afternoon.

I have lived half a fortnight, for the second time in as many weeks.

I no longer occasionally frequent dives.

Getting in a time machine and going back to visit yourself as a child can be very evocative.

The philosopher wouldn't come down to dinner because he hadn't got Time yet.

I had to make dentures for seven years.

If a man does not keep pace with his companions, perhaps it is because he has turf toe.

It ain't over till the fat lady has a stroke.

Never attempt to upbraid a woman whose hair is already up in a bun.

"One small step for a man. One giant leap for a man."

Vanity, vanity. Bathroom vanity.

It isn't whether you win or lose; it's location, location, location.

There are three keys to location: location, location, location.

It's time the government stopped catering to the people on Wall Street, and started looking out for the people on Raging Staph Infection Street.

Why don't they just have a deficit-cutting ceremony at the Lincoln Memorial and forget about it?

How can you tell if a gourd is truly American?

RIP, people of the 13th century.

Glucosamine and Chondroiten were famous generals who fought a great sea battle off the coast of Falafel in the 15th century. Not a lot of people know this.

Mary Rose was one of the first ships able to fire a broadside and was a firm favourite of King Henry VIII, described as, "the fairest flower of all the ships that ever sailed." The ship marked the transition between the medieval "floating castles" and the galleons of Elizabeth I's navy. On July 19, 1545, King Henry was at Southsea to watch the Mary Rose sally forth to engage French raiders. He ended up watching a disaster as the heavily laden Mary Rose keeled over in a squall of wind. The men's hearts sank along with the rest of their bodies as the Mary Rose rapidly capsized, water pouring into the lower gun ports. She had more than 90 guns on her decks at the time and her crew may have consisted of 700 members, of whom fewer than 40 are thought to have survived. That is still a lot of survivors considering that disaster happened nearly 500 years ago.

Sea battles are dramatic and all, but one wearies of these naval-gazing historians.

I'm ready. Just off the top of my head, Robespierre.

"Armed conflagration across three continents? The slaughter of countless millions? This means war!"

"The Redcoats are coming! The Redcoats are coming!" Paul cried as he rode into our history books, the most revered figure of the American Revolution.

QUOTES FROM FAMOUS PEOPLE

It behooves every man to remember that the work of the critic is of altogether secondary importance, and that, in the end, progress is accomplished by the man who does things.

— THEODORE ROOSEVELT

"Is it hot in here? I'm hot in here." —Winston Churchill

"Please, can you stop with that racket? I'm trying to think." —Albert Einstein

"Thank you, I'd love a shower. Absolutely." —Oscar Wilde

"There are clean towels on the dresser. Make yourself at home." —Mae West

"We're thinking about heading out in the morning." —Mother Theresa

"Mine is without the onions." —Dr. Martin Luther King, Jr.

"Did you change his diaper? Do I have to change his diaper?" —John Steinbeck

"People are living superficial, meaningless lives. More of them need to purchase Andrew Calhoun recordings." —Harriet Tubman

"Look, it's hot, I'm tired, my ass itches and we're not making any headway out here. Is that what you want to hear? Is it?" —Andrew Jackson.

"Turn left up here. No, right before the gas station." —Eleanor Roosevelt

"Oh man, that was amazing! I love you so much!" —Fyodor Dostoevsky

"We had a pretty good time yesterday. Sun was out, not too hot, just what you call pleasant." —Mahatma Gandhi

"I think I'm coming down with something." —Abraham Lincoln

"Wow, did you see that lady? That lady was really fat." —Chief Seattle

"Two of the cows are still out in the pasture." —Joan of Arc

PUNCTUATING MY REMARKS

Waltzing my ~

Had the baby di% out to be cleaned.

Jumpin' Jehoseph@!

Bring your & speakers

I don't care what happens. It's your *.

My mother and father both have PhD's. Would you like to see my ( )?

To _ my point, I made a — for the door.

. The end

THE
MEM
WARS
OF ANDREW CALHOUN

BY ANDY GOODMAN

THE TRILOGY TRILOGY

III
THE MEM WARS OF ANDREW CALHOUN TRILOGY
BY ANDY GOODMAN

And now (for I must rid my name of Ruth)
Behooves me speak the truth.

— DANTE ALIGHIERI

THE MEM WARS OF ANDREW CALHOUN TRILOGY
PART 1: THE EARLY YEARS AND THE SERIAL FOLKSINGER

I was born without a middle initial. My parents had to give me one— well, a middle name, really, from which the initial was derived.

Lord, I was born a ramblin' man. Well actually first I was a mewling and puking man. Then I was a crawling man. At last I took my first step, and my sister shouted, "Look! He's RAMBLING!! He's RAMBLING!!!"

My mother was still nursing me at age 3: it was a no-wean situation.

I traveled with my family when I was young, doing road theatre productions. My first roles were simply to be terrified of monsters; I was taught to yell "Eek!" and dash off stage. Times got rough and at one point Dad wanted to abandon me, but Mom convinced him that I was helping the family to eke out a living.

At that impressionable age, I didn't always know the difference between theatre and reality, and some of the stage monsters continue to haunt my dreaming and waking life to this day. My therapist diagnosed my condition as post-dramatic stress syndrome.

We were a three-generation theatrical family, beginning with my Grandpa, who wasn't so keen on me going into the life. He was a hard-boiled veteran who had lost his shirt in the Battle of

Dungarees, under the command of General Anesthesia. He enjoyed the military and applied for a job as minor-domo, but was discharged for medical reasons because he couldn't pass mustard.

So he got married and started a family. My grandmother and he had all their kids at once.

The first three quadruplets were delivered naturally, but a C-section became necessary when the last was not fourth coming.

They had been alerted that they might be having triplets, and had spent their last dime to purchase a triambulator from the Sears Catalog. My uncle Warren was odd man out, and he would be tied to the back by his feet and towed, banging along behind the others. No one knew there was anything wrong with this at the time, which accounts for all the descriptions of tow-headed boys in the literature of the day.

In the early days of the film industry, Hollywood was a cut-throat, dangerous place. Grandpa left because many of his thespian *compadres* were murdered by rivals. He had wearied of all the character actor assassination and innuendo.

We had one shotgun for family use, but Grandpa never left it in the same place twice. When we needed it, he couldn't remember where it was, so it fell to my brother Rod and me to scramble around and find it. On the occasion when the Johnson gang approached the house, I found it up against the outhouse wall, and went out to run them off with the oft-sought shotgun.

A couple years after he lost his teeth, Grandpa took up tap dancing. He said he figured he was already getting pretty good at the old soft chew.

Grandpa died before I was able to ask him why we called him "Chicken Oscar." I never asked my folks if they ever asked him either.

Maybe the following story will shed some light on this.

One of my formative experiences came when we were living in a housing project in Union, New Jersey, which was infested with rats. My father told me to respect the rats and leave them alone. But when no one was around, I would mock the rats and stick out my tongue at them. Eventually, one of them gave me quite the dressing down, calling me an "insufferable jackanapes." And that's the last time I gave a rat sass about anything whatsoever.

It was my mother's job to make posters for the theatrical shows, and in the days before computer printers, she would hand copy as many as seventy or eighty posters. She got so she could do it automatically while memorizing scenes or talking on the phone. Eventually she started to have problems with her wrists and shoulders. She went to the doctor, who diagnosed poster-automatic stress syndrome.

My sister and I used to make snow angels. The year she entered ninth grade, Leah announced that she would no longer engage in child splay.

In middle school I met a kid named John Family. Being the two shortest kids in the school, we naturally gravitated toward one another. We used to play Crazy Eights in the cafeteria. One day he asked me, "Hey, you want to play 52 Pick-up?" "What's that?"— I asked, and he threw my deck of cards on the floor. Was I ever impressed! We became great friends. He did apologize years later when we were grown up, saying "I'm sorry I was short with you back when we were in Junior High."

His folks had a place on a lake in Wisconsin where we'd go for long weekends. The Family family was like family to me.

They picked up an imp figure at Lana's Lawn Ornaments. It stood on their front lawn in all seasons, demonstrating the concept of imp permanence.

Family's Dad was a hard-working family man. He owned and operated the Family Family Restaurant, but he hired a weekend manager so he could spend time with family. Usually a very cautious, law-abiding driver, he'd get all keyed up on Fridays when he was trying to get the family up to their vacation property through the weekend traffic.

Due to his weekend condition, Mr. Family died of a sudden heart attack. The family took his ashes up to bury at the Lake. They figured he'd urned a vacation.

John's aunt Andrea was a church deacon. As she lit candles for the service, she whispered a secret. I took it as a votive confidence.

Mr. Family had hoped to be remembered for his rather wretched etchings, but it turns out that his biggest legacy was his chicken fricassee recipe, which is still served at the Family Family Restaurant. The place is under different ownership now. They put on an addition for expanded seating, and changed the name to the Family Family Restaurant Restaurant.

When I drove by the Family place thirty years later, the imp was still in position in the front yard. It seemed improbable, so I stole it.

John Family now owns a men's accessories shop in the Yorktown mall, called Family Ties.

My first crush was on this cute Scandinavian pig-tailed girl named Heidi. I'd already read and loved the book "Heidi," and she seemed like she'd stepped right out of the pages of that book. Looking back, I think maybe I had it backwards: Did I really love Heidi, or was I merely in love with the idieH of Heidi?

My big brother Rod was a chess fanatic. Mom and Dad felt he was making it an obsession and took away his chess set. When they weren't around he'd make me squat on all fours and draw the squares on my back, setting up make-shift pieces so he could ponder his moves. If I moved and caused a piece to fall, he'd strike me with a mattock.

Our high school had all four years' wrestling matches simultaneously in the gym, putting out mats in a rectangle. Then they added in the eighth graders as well, going from a four-mat format to a five-mat format.

Being habitually stuck in bottom position due to post-Rod mattock chess syndrome, I was an indifferent wrestler. My self-esteem at that time came from my natural ability with poetry and lore. It was then that I came to be known as the No-Holds Bard.

Despite this I was a poor English student and never cared much for punctuation, which ultimately redounded to my benefit in my work as a comma derider for the Anti Punctuation League.

I saw "Sunday" misspelled "Sundand" in my youth, and have been haunted by it ever since. Thoughts such as "We watch Butch Cassidy and the Sundand Kid every Sundand" are never far away. I hope this will not become a problem for *you.*

My family drifted out of the theatre. Not any one particular theatre. We drifted out of the performing theatre world altogether. Dad was offered the role of the giant in *Jack and the Beanstalk.* They said there was no fee involved, and he didn't think "fi fo fum" was going to cut it.

Looking back, I think I was just tired of all the drama.

My parents sent me to work on a dairy farm for the summer. Farmer Fritz was to teach me to herd and milk his prized Guernseys in exchange for room and board and fresh air.

He told me if I counted the cows and listed them by name, he'd give me seventy-five cents a day. There was no paper, so I wrote the list on my body, thus becoming a cattle list for change.

I'd then multiply the number of cows by four to get the number of functional teats. This, along with the good fresh milk, inspired my lifetime practice of teat totaling.

I was a tender-hearted kid, and one day I accidentally dug up some baby rabbits. They were then abandoned by their mother, and the old farmer told me to suckle them. "There," he said, "That'll put hares on your chest!"

A son of immigrants in Delavan, WI, Farmer Fritz had spent years developing a new type of cheese, working with different processing methods and breeds of cow; at last he came up with a soft, textureless cheese that smelled like an old dishrag: naming it for his maternal grandfather Orzach, he sent it to be registered with the dairy board. They declined his new category, saying "I'm afraid you've created a Muenster."

As much as I enjoyed the farm, it made the adjustment to school all the more difficult. The popular kids began to call me "Cow-hoon." "I'm gonna pound you, Cow-hoon..." they intoned, as if aggrieved that my existence had made such an activity necessary.

Fritz' farm was acquired by a large conglomerate, which retained him, retraining him for a position in middle management. He gave me a heads up that I would be invited to come on board as a team member, saying he valued my skill set in getting on the same page with the competitive, highly efficient Guernseys. Somehow the notion of spending my life on a corporate dairy farm was udderly draining. Telling Farmer Fritz that the position did not fit my needs at that time, I determined to leave the cows behind and moo forward with my plans.

Naturally I set my sights on a career in Farm Ecology. But the initial courses were nothing but drugs, drugs, drugs. So, I decided to become a musician.

I became a folksinger because I have ineptitude for music.

I still get butterflies in my stomach before I perform. Usually with a little mayonnaise and dill.

Lord, how I've rambled.

Lemme tell ya about it:

> Oh I am the rovin' rambler
> Who roams from town to town
> Wherever I go to bed at night,
> That's where I lay me down
>
> Yes I'm a weary wanderer
> Upon my odyssey
> Some call me a sojourner,
> An itinerant man, that's me

Yes I've traveled through glen and meadow
I've marched through meadow and glen
And again through glen and meadow
And meadow and glen again

I've paced o'er gully and mesa
I've hiked through hill and dale
Through wind and sleet and rain and snow
And fire and storm and gale

Roving, roving,
Rambling down the road

I've strolled o'er mountains and deserts
Set forth from shore to shore
I've trekked the frozen tundra
And heard the ocean's roar

I've plodded through the jungle
I've trodden through the veldt
I've traipsed through subterranean caves
Traversing the land of the Celt

I've ambled through Australia
Gallivanted through Guam
Took a junket to Jamaica
Ventured through Viet Nam

I've knocked about the Midlands
And ranged the Pyrenees
Surveyed the Siberian desert
And voyaged on to Greece

Roving, roving,
Rambling down the road

From the hills of Madagascar
To Everest's mighty peak
From the racetracks of Nascar
To the coast of Mozambique

I've oft commuted from Norway
To the cities of Peru
I did it my way and your way
I'd nothing better to do

As I cruised from ports of Chile
Up to old Brazil
On a ship en route to China
You'll find me faring still

I hie up the Himalayas
Then head to old Ukraine
Yes on my peregrinations
I schlepp through France and Spain

Roving, roving,
Rambling down the road

I gad about the Galapagos
And stride through old Japan
Meandering through Canada
A circumforaneous man

So you can call me a nomad
A vagrant or a bum
As I saunter down the highway
Holding out my thumb

Yet I'll remain a drifter
I'm here and then I'm gone
But I can sing no more today
I must be moving on

If anyone should ask of me
Please tell them if you can
I'm a tramping itinerant rover
A peripatetic man.

Rovin', rovin',
Ramblin' down the road.*

---

* "The Itinerant Rover" by Andrew Calhoun

You know what they say. Some nights you eat the bear, some nights you don't eat the bear.

I married young, sired offspring (see *The Mem Wars of Andrew Calhoun Trilogy II),* and took any gig I could get to support the family.

Sometimes the only feedback I got was from the PA system.

One night after I'd played at a Ground Round in Morton Grove for 10 minutes the manager told me to stop because a road club had arrived with their own microphone and wanted to have a meeting. He pre-empted my performance, paying me $25 of the promised $40. I learned never to play at places named after hamburger.

One night John Benischek called me to fill in for him at "Uncle Dan's Second Story" in Peotone, Illinois. I carried my sturdy Martin D-28 along with my fragile hopes and dreams of artistic recognition into a smoky room displaying Navy insignia and a large painting of an ungainly nude behind the bar. It became apparent over the course of the night that my songs had no particular appeal to the people of Peotone. I played three sets to zero applause. The owner said "Well it didn't go so well" and paid me $30 rather than the expected $50.

At least he didn't send me home early.

There were good gigs too, and plentiful opportunities to play at local festivals, pizza joints, bars, coffeehouses, corn roasts, folk clubs, fern bars and restaurants of every sort. But nobody really earns a living as a folksinger. Most of us sold products on the side, or married professional people.

I reveal here for the first time the "coded songs" of the greater Chicago folk scene. When a folksinger played "City of New Orleans," it was a signal to those in the know that the artist was an Amway representative; if it were "Mr. Bojangles," that performer was dealing from a trunk full of Mason shoes. Shaklee vitamin distributors would alert the cognoscenti with sensitive renditions of "The Dutchman." "Satisfied Mind" meant the singer was available for the night, for a price. The nostalgic strains of "The Roseville Fair" belied its offer of the key to a house of profligacy so vile and degenerate that relating its nature is beyond the scope even of this book.

I didn't care to perform any of these songs, so in order to supplement my income, I began to write popular fiction. My self-published first novel was a Western tale entitled *The Unbehoven*.

I'd ordered and paid for bound books; but they came in the scroll binding, the kind I could have done myself at a copy shop. I sued, but the court ruled that the plastic scroll was, legally, binding.

Friends were sympathetic, many sending the identical Hallmark card, with "I'm sorry for your lawsuit" inscribed over the bas-relief scales of justice.

A literary agent, Louise Forrestal, approached me after a gig at The Great American Coffeehouse.

She let me know how impressed she was by *The Unbehoven* and offered to represent me. I'm not sure how she ever ran across it, illustrating how what appears to be a disaster can sometimes lead to greater things.

Louise was a hard-boiled veteran of the publishing business, more concerned about having a stable of writers who could churn out pulp under a deadline than she was about our pretensions to literary quality. She found me steady work ghostwriting novels and non-fiction of various sorts. Sometimes I published under my mother's maiden name of Goodman. Yes, for those of you who have only known me when I'm wearing my folksinger "hat," yes, I'm Andy Goodman. Hi!

In summer of 1980 I did a one-minute audition for Mayor Byrne's Summertime Chicago program. It was then illegal for street musicians to perform for tips in the city, so they hired people who could sing and/or play loudly for the stipend of $150 a week. We were scheduled morning and evening rush hours from 6:30-9 a.m. and 4:30-6 p.m., and given transportation passes. Some of the 6:30

gigs were at remote bus stops on the Southwest side, which took me well over an hour to get to, involving two transfers. We were to wear "Mayor Byrne's Summertime Chicago" T-shirts, and set up our "Mayor Byrne's Summertime Chicago" styrofoam folding display boards. Often I'd be scheduled twice daily at busy bus stops or subways in the Loop. To commuters hustling through the cacophony, I may as well have been miming "Will the Circle Be Unbroken" or "Reilly's Daughter" with the puffing buses lining up or long rush hour trains rumbling in from both directions.

That same summer I was under contract at King Richard's Faire, a Renaissance festival near Bristol, Wisconsin, weekends, performing in hat, doublet, breeches and tights. After three or four weeks of borderline heat prostration, I ditched the tights, put on a kilt and played the Scot.

After singing manfully to buses and trains all week I soldiered on through the weekend swelter, regaling passersby with Scottish ballads on their way to the swordsman's show, or the turkey legs, or the fried ice cream, or the joust.

Mike Cross' song "The Scotsman" originated as a joke about a drunken Scot lying asleep in the grass who is stumbled upon by two lasses. They peer beneath his kilt and tie a blue ribbon to "the bonny star"; when he wakes to nature's call and finds the ribbon, he says, "Lad, I don't know where ye been, but I see ye won first prize!" It's rounded out with a rousing "Ring ding diddle diddle-i-dee-O!" chorus. It's a popular song at Renaissance fairs, whose loyal patrons herd in year after year to be amused by the same tittie and weenie jokes.

Late one scorching, humid August day, a woman came and sat on the bench in front of me and was the first that summer to request of me "The Scotsman.'"

I was already playing the Scotsman. I wouldn't ask a Dutchman to play "The Dutchman," or a Southern man to play "Southern Man."

A summer's frustration and heat and dust had gone to my head. "I *hate* that song," I snapped, breaking character. Taken aback and looking slightly confused, she rose and strode in the direction of the Mud Beggars.

Just a few minutes later, three beer-swillers came by demanding I "Play 'The Scotsman!'" "I don't know it! You want to hear '*The Jew*?!' It's making fun of a guy in a yarmulke!"

I enjoy a good joke. The one about hamsters and duct tape is one of my favorites. But I wouldn't make a song out of it. And if I did, I wouldn't ask a hamster dressed in duct tape to sing it.

What I didn't understand at the time, what not one among my musical *compadres* at the Faire had clued me in on, was that "The Scotsman" was one of the coded songs.

In 1981, I was working my first two-week stint for decent pay at *The Abbey*, a fine Irish Pub then at the corner of Addison and Narragansett on Chicago's West Side. Four sets a night, Wednesday through Saturday. It being in the month of January, I caught the flu during the first week. Pounding out "The Wild Rover" and "The Irish Rover" and "The Moonshiner," became a noisome chore. The Irish pub style at that time was to embellish each line with the Tommy Makem *hump*, punching the first syllable for emphasis. This was not how folk songs were traditionally performed down through the centuries in the Emerald Isle. When the Clancy Brothers and Tommy Makem brought their treasury of old songs Stateside in the early sixties, they found to their dismay that Americans had the attention spans of goldfish. The Brothers and Tommy donned matching fisherman's sweaters and hyped up the material to adapt it to the lowest common denominator, adding banjo and pumping their fists in the air. Unfortunately, the style caught on and there was no turning back. By Saturday night I had a fever topping a hundred and one and had to force my voice through the phlegm dripping through my vocal cords until I wasn't singing with my voice so much as with the damage done to it, rasping out "AND it's No, Nay, Never" to the milling throng. Somehow, I made it. Through the night, through the week, through all four sets, through that last interminable chorus of "The Parting Glass." I was relieving myself at the urinal when the owner came in and stood beside me, sharing a moment, and said, "You know it's *five* sets on Saturday night, don'tcha?"

A professional entertainer must learn to field requests. My method is, "Sorry, I don't know that one." A gentleman came up at a restaurant gig in West Dundee and requested "Amy." "Sorry, I don't know that one." "That's an acoustic piece," he said, shaking his head disapprovingly. So is "La Marseillaise," I suppose. Neil Young fans in drinking establishments are a breed unto themselves; they refuse to accept that you don't know any "*NEIL YOUNG!!!— NEIL YOUNG!!!*"— and continue to howl like lost souls for Neil between songs until the night is over. If you know a Neil song or two, by all means sing it. But don't expect them to stop screaming at you. Rates of recidivism to "*NEIL YOUNG!!!— NEIL YOUNG!!!*" are off the charts. A patron at another restaurant gig approached the stage, interrupting the dénouement of Leonard Cohen's "Famous Blue Raincoat" with a request for "Peaceful Easy Feeling." I trace the germination of my homicidal tendencies to that moment.

There are those nights that fill the sails, when you really feel like you're connecting with people, sharing from your life, pouring your heart out, dredging up angels and demons in song, faithful to the muse, sparing nothing. And those nights, a man will come up after listening to all this with flat staring fish-eyes, and say:

"What kind of guitar is that?"

I wonder if people have approached Nureyev or Martha Graham or Baryshnikov after dance performances, still gasping for air and streaming with sweat, and asked "What kind of leotard is that?" Or approached Dylan Thomas or Toni Morrison after a reading and asked, "What weight paper is your book printed on?" There's just something about the guitar thing. It is almost always a man alone, approaching retirement age, who has an urgent desire to know what kind of guitar I'm playing.

I began murdering those people. I'm not proud of it. But that's part of the story— those guys, asking "What kind of guitar is that?"— winding up in dumpsters and highway ditches and shallow graves around the country. My first kill was in Ottumwa, IA, in 1981. I had to cut him up to get him into a thirty-gallon Hefty Bag to leave in the freezer in the basement of Auntie Peete's Bar and Grille. I can't imagine these people have families, or friends, as I've managed to off seventy-eight of them and, with the rare exceptions noted below, no one has ever taken notice of their disappearance.

My second book, a moderate small press success under my own name, was called *Going Brogue: My Years As An Irish Folksinger.*

A hobby cum research project on spelunking led to the writing of *Caving,* an underground classic.

I ghostwrote *The Missing Disc,* by Pierce Vertebra, third in a series of spine novels set in the Lumbar Region of Southern France.

Up in Smoke, a book about the history of chimney construction followed— sales were through the roof!

The Forty-Niners, a tale of the California gold rush, was panned. This was my first book deal with Harcourt, Brace Yourself Bridget & Company, and of course we were all very disappointed.

—*∿*—

My first self-help book, *Healing Self and Community* by Andy Goodman, suggested one thing people can do to develop their spirituality and connect with their communities, is to present house concerts by touring folksingers. There was a chapter on this with a set of workshop questions in the back.

I like to think I'm a pretty decent writer, but I can't say I've really written anything comparable to *The Bible,* or *War and Peace,* or even *The Collected Works of William Shakespeare.*

The road takes its toll. It's been easier since the advent of the I-Pass.

There's a physical toll to be paid as well. Your car wears out. Your back goes out.

Sometimes old hip injuries come back to haunch you.

I continued to ramble, as indeed I had since birth, mining the untolled riches of America's back roads.

The eighties saw the first stirrings of the "house concert." They call them "house shows" in some parts of the country, which I guess is fine, although the "s" into "sh" sound doesn't scan as well; and some will say "home shows," a phrase evoking the shrill, gloomy resonance of a bowed psaltery. I, for one, prefer the crisp, distinct clarity of "the house concert," thank you very much. I did a week of those in Wisconsin, six in seven days, calling to book dates with total strangers willing to welcome a folk singing Blanche Dubois into their homes to entertain their friends and relations, and stay overnight.

It took just a moment upon arrival to get a sense of how the gigs would go. This was a time of widespread wall-to-wall carpeting, a first bad sign; people with crew cut lawns and molded shrubs and spotless, antiseptic homes open the door and then step back while their Doberman/pit bull mix burrows relentlessly into your crotch as you try to make your hello; you twist and shimmy but cannot avoid the determined thrusts of the malevolent animal. You attempt to block him out with your guitar case but embarrassment escalates into terror as he growls and crouches and barks menacingly, eyes burning with implacable hatred; the host will feign surprise at Tinker's ever acting this way, and finally drag him off, while welcoming you and apologizing for the messy house. You then get "the tour of the house," including the basement rec room with its pool table and wet bar. This sort of host has precious few books, all of which are of the self- or home-improvement variety; higher culture is represented by a couple of seascape reproductions complementing the living room set and the ubiquitous Norman Rockwell picture of a kid taking a shit, displayed on the bathroom walls of such homes. Their actual kids are relegated to the rec room during your performance, occasional shrieks and television noise seeping up the back stairs during the show. There is a gleaming piano there beside you with a *Pop Hits* book published twenty years ago with no crease in its binding. You, like the seascapes, piano and songbook, are just for show. This is neither a generous nor a purchasing crowd. If you like chain pizza and M&Ms, fill up.

Another sort of host has wall-to-wall books, with throw rugs, stacks of magazines and papers and instruments and paintings comprising a grand mess similar to that in your own house, for which they notably do not apologize. There is no tour of the house after you've been shown your room, but their children will show you what they're into and sit and enjoy the show with their parents, who do not send them to bed until after the show. Books are involved with bedtime, and if you are very lucky you will be invited to read. The painting you like enough to comment on was given to them by the artist, a friend. A bottle of single malt appears around midnight, accompanied by gut-busting jokes and welcome soul talk about real things. You did well with the basket and sales and accept an invitation to return. It was at one of these midnight bull sessions that a former Renaissance Faire juggler and fire-eater cum Philosophy Professor at the University of Nebraska told me the real meaning of "The Scotsman."

All hosts say, "There are clean towels on the dresser." I've never had a dirty one left out for me, but appreciate the reassurance nonetheless. Some hosts have awaiting you in their guest room, eighty-seven pillows, covering two thirds of the bed, to be laboriously removed before sleeping. This helps us to stay in shape on the road.

When I started touring, one perk of the road was the opportunity to try so many sensually appealing types of shampoo: Herbal Essence, Pantene, Wella Balsam, Breck, Prell, Pert, Suave, White Rain, Agree, Halsa, with stimulating infusions of coconut, apricot, vanilla, apple, lemon, citrus, aloe and clove in cornucopious variety. When I was a child in the early sixties there was, simply, shampoo. My mother would dig a slightly metallic smelling turquoise cream out of a white jar and scrub our heads, her powerful fingers reshaping our heads during this process so no one would know we were Jewish. It was an innocent time in many ways. Generally back in the late seventies, there would be two bottles. You had the shampoo on the one hand and the conditioner on the other hand. Then there was an historic moment of pure unity remembered now only by a remnant few, of shampoo and conditioner in one bottle, sitting on the sill. We as a society have strayed from this ideal. When I step into a host's shower it can take several minutes to search through sprawling bottles of body washes, shower gels, body scrubs, conditioner, conditioner, conditioner, conditioner, shampoo for people who color their hair, shampoo for people of color who perm their hair, dog shampoo, beard conditioner oil and so on before I find the regular old normal, dry, or oily shampoo. I'm not particular. But this one bottle is empty. I wrap up in a towel and dance gingerly back to my room to get my own shampoo, which I had neglected to grab in the first place from my suitcase. I realize now that I left it behind in the last town. Once again I will be forced to shampoo with body wash.

The house concert audience will bring a multitude of cookies and brownies, most of which remain at the end of the night. The hosts usually bag this up and give it to the artist to take with them. This is what folksingers mean by "bringing home the bakin'."

I played for years at a center for street alcoholics on skid row in Chicago's Uptown; I walked through Alphabet Land in lower Manhattan, stepping with guitar and suitcase over heroin addicts to get into buildings; though I've driven through roiling mad traffic in Boston and Detroit, roulette wheel cloverleafs in Los Angeles and San Francisco, Chicago blizzards and blind zero-to-sixty merges in New York City, my most terrifying experiences occurred in seemingly sedate rural areas.

Once I stayed with a family of Burgesses on a communal farm in Minnesota who had their open toilet on the landing between floors. One required to move their bowels would thus be visible from anywhere in the house. Norman Rockwell strikes again. "We may as well live our nightmares," I suppose is the philosophy. Strong folks.

My Scottish ancestors used to sit playing "The Crapping Reel" on the small pipes while squatting wi their kilts hoisted up beside a gorse bush, awaiting relief. My Jewish forebears engaged in similar practices. King Saul, for example, in *Judges 3:24*:

"When he was gone out, his servants came; and when they saw that, behold, the doors of the parlour *were* locked, they said, Surely he covereth his feet in his summer chamber."

There is fossil evidence of humans having bowel movements even prior to Biblical times. Defecation is believed by anthropologists to be nearly universal amongst the races of humanity. So it's not so much that I mind crapping in front of people. At the end of the day, I'm a performer. It's that I just really don't want to wipe my ass in front of them. Some things, even in our current world of disintegration of the traditional values of church and family, are sacred. I waited to get to a gas station "summer chamber" on the way out of town the next morning.

I drove on to a lofty, open wooden house back in the northwestern Wisconsin woods that Barry and Judy had built themselves. They offered me black bean salad with mango and cilantro and gave me the tour of the place. Only one neighbor lady came for the show. I think they really just wanted to show me their house. I had to climb a frightfully steep ladder to my sleeping loft, and there was no railing up there, so if you were, say, a sleepwalker, or even a little careless getting up in the night, it would have been a long fall to their beautifully polished broad beam floor.

Indeed it was. They found me crumpled up in the morning, with all the ribs of my left side cracked, my head split open and my right leg skewed at a hideous angle. I know this because they sent me a picture of it later, along with one of me posing smiling with Barry in front of the house at the time of my arrival, along with views of their home's upper beam construction, adapted flying buttresses, wet bar, well house and flower garden.

I was rushed to the hospital in Eau Claire, where they did triage to stop the bleeding and helicoptered me on to Abbot Northwestern hospital in Minneapolis.

I went in for anthropomorphic surgery. I was thus empowered to discuss philosophy and higher mathematics with the likes of moles and alligators.

Due to tightening budgets and my lack of health insurance, I was shorted on the anesthesia and kept drifting in and out of consciousness during the surgery. The surgeons maintained a continual banter.

"Aren't you cutting it a little close?"

"Are you asking me or telling me?"

"Are you arguing with me?"

"Am I arguing? I'm not arguing."

"Oh, cripes, Jake. See what you made me do?"

"You take the tendon from the other leg. He'll never know the difference."

When I was in the recovery room the nurse kept bringing cups of ice, but the fever never broke. Sometimes ice chips aren't all they're cracked up to be.

The first dose of aspirin helped, but just Bayerly.

The nurse brought more, explaining that if you have to take an aspirin, sometimes it's good to take it with a little aspirin.

I applied for extensive physical therapy. The hospital said that they could only offer an abbreviated rehabilitation. So I said, okay then, rehab.

I learned a lot about life from that experience. But due to the brain injury, I can't remember what it is.

One thing I have retained. Now when hosts offer the tour of the house, I take it with great interest, commenting with particular appreciation on the impressive weekend warrior-crafted wet bar. After they leave me alone in my room a couple minutes, I toss my suitcase out the window, hoist my guitar in the gig bag, slide down the drainpipe and pull out of the driveway before they know I'm gone. It's just less trouble for everyone.

———〰———

After my first LP, *The Essential Genius of Andrew Calhoun* was released on Premierre in 1983, I began to get some college bookings through an agency which "launched" me on a national tour. One of the better college gigs left over from what U. Utah Phillips dubbed the "folk scare" of the sixties was SUNY Geneseo, about an hour east of Buffalo. This was a two night, $450 booking and reports were that it was a great gig with a long track record of exciting shows from important artists and there would be a full house. There I was preparing to be important, going over songs for the gig in my room in the Student Union when the chair of the coffeehouse committee knocked on the door. She was wearing a T-shirt that said "Run" with wavy lines. Apparently not a Tact major, she said, "Nobody comes to the coffeehouse anymore. I guess they just don't like coffeehouse performers." And she looked at me wistfully.

So I wrote and sang:

> Nobody comes to the coffeehouse,
> Nobody comes to the coffeehouse,
> Nobody comes to the coffeehouse,
> Folksingers are boring.

> Chorus:
> Boring, boring, boring, so boring,
> Nobody comes to the coffeehouse,
> Folksingers are boring.

> (Chorus)

> First they start some silly song,
> Try to make you sing along,
> Always drag it out too long:
> Folksingers are boring.

> (Chorus)

First they sing a song about a train,
Then they sing a song about a train,
Then they sing a song about a train:
Folksingers are boring.

(Chorus)

Folksingers have flabby buns,
They all play the same bass runs,
They're against the private ownership of handguns:
Folksingers are boring.

(Chorus)

Folksingers are born to lose,
They wear old and ratty shoes,
Then they try to sing the blues:
Then they're really boring.

(Chorus)

Give us salsa, give us soul,
Give us good old rock and roll,
Pass the bong and pass the bowl
Folksingers are boring.

(Chorus)
(Chorus)
(Chorus)

The coffeehouse chair and six audience members sang along, linking arms and swaying back and forth together. I'd had the honor of closing out a few venues and concert series: now I would signal the death throes of a genre.

The folkie college circuit along with the urban folk club scene was indeed moribund by the mid-eighties.

Folk music, however, sees more resurrections than Bugs Bunny. Generally we re-ignite the base with a dirge for a passing way of life. Like "Fifteen Years on the Erie Canal" eulogizing the mule-barge or "City of New Orleans" lamenting the locomotive,

"Folksingers are Boring," mourned the passing of the folk boom. At first performed by folksingers (Harvey Reid learned it in one hearing at the Pressroom in New Hampshire), it was printed in *Sing Out!* Magazine and picked up by punk and rock artists, crossing over into mainstream pop and country markets: translated into dozens of languages, it was sung even behind the iron curtain. Some credit the dissolution of the Soviet Union to the throngs bravely linking arms, swaying and singing "Folksingers are Boring" in a grand protest in Palace Square in St. Petersburg in February of 1987. I was invited to sing it at the White House, but as then President Reagan was taking credit for the collapse of "The Evil Empire," I sent my peremptory regrets.

The house concert circuit burgeoned in the nineties. It became possible to make one's way across the country with only an occasional club or bar gig. I enjoyed my first trip across the Rocky Mountains in 1996. I did a show with a nice family in Boulder, the Ramseys. They had a pretty little girl, precociously coquettish, dressed up like a beauty queen at age 6, very demure. There was a good crowd of enthusiastic, well-heeled folks; CD sales were brisk during the break. To get a rise out of the little girl in the second set, I mixed in some surefire kids songs— "The Fox," "This Little Light of Mine," "The Hole in the Bottom of the Sea,"— yet could not engage her to sing or clap along. I went farther out on a limb with a shameless performance of Tom Paxton's asinine "The Marvelous Toy." There was still no response from her on that, and a bare smattering of polite applause from the adults. The night was irredeemable. I finished up on autopilot, chafing inwardly. Audience members were already beginning to leave as I phoned in "The Streets of London." With curt smiles, the remainder evaporated rapidly into the night. The little girl came up and asked:

"What kind of guitar is that?"

Shortly thereafter I released *Figs,* my finest album to date.

A few months after 9/11, in a motel in Marion, VA, I finally solved the mystery of my Grandpa's sobriquet. I was watching classic boxing on HBO. First up was a hard-fought 1975 bout with

"The Dictator," Baby Doc Duvalier, falling to "The Irish Hammer," Peen O'Shea, in 11 rounds. Then came a fight from 1951: "Chicken" Oscar Goodman vs. "Shrimp" Louie Katorz. Grandpa was flapping his arms around, flailing and jabbing away for 14 rounds until the little guy from Newark laid him out. Chicken Oscar had to be carried out in a styrofoam container. Shrimp Louie had taken one too many one-two punches to the head and had to be carried out as well. It was said that the fight brought a new dimension to the sport: carry-out boxing.

My first children's book, by Andy Goodman with illustrations by Walt Bannerman, was published in 2004. *The Intrepid Potato* re-imagines the classic hero's journey for youngsters aged 7 to 9: the virgin birth, the ostracism, the overcoming of trials, and the triumphant return, with chives.

The enduring attraction of the road, apart from the readily available oral sex for those willing to sing "The Scotsman," is the friends along the way.

A few years back I was playing doubles hide and seek with my songwriter pals down in Austin. It was me and Karen Mal vs. Danny Schmidt and Carrie Elkin. Danny and Carrie were hot on our trail, so we dashed into one of my regular hiding places— M. Balmer's Funeral Home, where I knew of a place I could crawl in under the counter. "Aye, M.," I said, "have you got a place for Mal to hide?" "There's two caskets right here. Jump on in!" One was a smooth pine casket, the other, knotty oak. "Swirls before pine," said Karen, and hid like a little chick inside the oak. The Balmers were impressed that she could be so quiet while she was in their coffin.

I've played hide and seek with many well-known people. At one time I played doubles with Margaret Chase Smith, Michael Smith and Paul Tagliabue.

I spent a few highly focused years in the specific Northwest.

I grew a ponytail to prepare for my impending stewardship of the earth.

I enjoyed living in Portland, but simply could not abide waiters and waitresses sitting down insouciantly at one's table to take one's order. I found such behavior to be forward, lazy, and impertinent. I made a life decision at that time to move back to the Midwest.

After that I was in the mob for a while, but found it to be riddled with corruption— payoffs and the like.

Taciturn by nature, I joined the National Association of Real Terse.

I thought I was a pretty good songwriter, but ultimately I turned out to be just another shill for the big insurance companies— no big surprise there.

THE MEM WARS OF ANDREW CALHOUN TRILOGY
PART 2: MARRIAGE(S), CHILDREN AND
THE VOYAGE OF SELF-DISCOVERY

The eagle's bird hath spread his wings,
And from far off hath taken flight,
In which mean way by no leverings
On bough or branch this bird would light;
Till on the rose, both red and white,
He 'lighteth now most lovingly,
And thereto most behovingly.

— JOHN HEYWOOD

What a difference a dame makes.

My first wife, Bertice, thought I hung the moon. Must have been those lunary clips I left lying around.

She was a fine artist, but made her living as a nurse. She drew blood with a pencil.

I was having a full-blown manic episode when we met, which made me appear to be relatively normal.

She asked me over for coffee and I undressed her with my eyes. It took a long time, as the eyelids are clumsy with buttons.

We began to take baths together, and didn't discuss the occasional air bubble unless it came up naturally.

Bertice and I had two kids of course, twins, and we named them Hannah and Boy.

Kids grow up fast. One day I got the toddlers ready for a stroll. But they no longer fit the prameters.

Hannah enjoyed spending time with people in her own H group.

She showed an early interest in Psychology, so we signed her up for "Jungsters," where the kids were encouraged to mold archetypal figures from the collective unconscious out of Play Doh.

But Boy was solitary. Boy, was he.

I can tell you this, because the little son of a gun has never taken the least interest in my writing and he'll never read this anyway: we're not sure he's ours. Bertice left him for a moment at one of the baby changing stations at a highway oasis in Ohio, and thinks another mother may have swapped him out.

We went to parent/teacher conferences. Teacher told us Boy had gradeability. We said, "So? And?!?" "Well sometimes we just question whether your boy Boy is being as capable as he's capable of being."

He was suspended from intramural hockey because he threw his hat in the rink.

Boy was what you might call suggestible. He had no concept of metaphor. After a kid at school said "Put your money where your mouth is," he began to keep all of his dimes and quarters we gave him for school lunch in his cheek.

He became obsessed with the Cubs/Braves pitcher, Greg Maddux. He had a poster of him in his room and used to stare at it for hours. He asked for a Greg Maddux jersey for his birthday, and wore it continually. Then he started asking us to call him Greg. Bertice grew short with him; "You have a perfectly good name that your father gave you. Your name is Boy." And he wept.

We took him to see a therapist, who diagnosed him with poster-Maddux dress syndrome.

He said his suggestibility issue was due to a new disorder endemic among Northern Illinois pre-teens who were too careful to obey external direction; and due to this our Boy was *overheeding*.

Dr. Infantino told him he should try to get a grip on himself. After that Boy spent all his time masturbating in his room.

I suggested he might attenuate his compulsive behavior. "Boy, moderation in everything— including masturbation."

He parried of course with a quote from Homer: "It behooves a father to be blameless if he expects his child to be."

We signed him up for Little League. He turned out to be the team's best pitcher as well as the teams' best hitter, earning two trophies. The need to display them side by side became paramount.

Concerned about our communication issues, I took him along fishing. He affected a sullen silence, and after a while I asked him to bait the hook. Boy said, "Look, I didn't come out here to open up a can of worms."

We all enjoyed the Star Trek movie. It was fascinating to me, with my theatre background, to think about how the whole thing was put together behind the scenes. I was impressed that they used actual Romulan and Vulcan people to play those characters. That's what you can do when you've got the big budget!

We thought about pets. A costly proposition: purchase price of the animal; food, shots, kitty litter, leashes and runs and chew toys, carrying boxes, vet bills; funeral expenses. Do you know what it costs to neuter a newt?

Boy wanted an orange tomcat, so we set out to acquire several females, as we'd heard cats were supposed to have nine wives.

Both kids began clamoring for a pug. There was an ad in the paper; a couple in Rockford said they had a litter and the puppies were in our price range. I was going out to pick one up, but was glad I called first. The lady told me they were already six weeks sold. So we got a mutt, half pit bull and half pugnacious.

Pets ruled our lives. It was reigning cats and dogs.

Hannah's venerable hamster Harry was injured by one of the cats reaching into his cage. We took him down to the vet, who sent us on to the small rodent specialist in Orland Park. Dr. Carlisle said she actually had (he told us Harry was a female), an advanced hamster cancer in addition to the protruding intestines. He said he could operate, but it would cost $7800 plus food and lodging and there was no guarantee that "Hamster Calhoun" would survive the surgery. Dr. Carlisle took me aside and said he'd be glad to do the work but suggested it probably wasn't the best investment. He offered to put Harry down for a $75 fee. There comes a time when a man needs to set an example of grace under pressure for his children. "Fuck you!" I screamed, slapping his glasses off his face and snatching our beleaguered rodent from the table. "We'll deal with this ourselves." When we got home I put some tequila in a little glass and then fed her from the dropper. I don't know if it comforted Harry but I figured it was worth a shot. Hannah put a bandage on the wound, and, to our amazement, the hamster recovered fully. All of the family pets from that time have gone on, but Harry is still with us, cancer-free, still running on the wheel and just beginning to slow down, twenty-five years later.

When the kids were younger, Bertice was unhappy with the amount of time my touring life took from the family. We opened a little shop on Greenleaf Street so I could spend more time at home. I wanted to call it "Gifts and Shit," but Bertice wanted to go with "Greenleaf Gifts." I've often wondered if the business might still be thriving and how all of our lives would have turned out differently if we'd gone with one or the other, rather than compromising on "Greenleaf Gifts and Shit."

The rest of the kids' teen years, it's not that they were uneventful. Let's just say that the problem with teenagers is that they tend to be juvenile. It seems intemperate anger is all the rage. We did instill in our children the core value that decapitating family members is inappropriate.

To date, Boy hasn't been able to turn his bachelor's degree in foyers into gainful employment. So he's going to graduate school to become a lobbyist.

Hannah excelled in typing, but said she didn't think she could handle the rigors of secretarial work. I advised her that, though data entry can be tedious and time-consuming, persistence will out. You've just got to keypad it.

She went in for anthropology and did field work studying canoodling patterns among lemurs.

She calls it bad luck but I'm afraid that Hannah has made some poor relationship choices. We think she may have a dude misorder.

She dated Oney Orenstein, a guy trying to get a gig writing for Marvel Comics. He was developing a super-hero who was able to make himself *incredibly* tiny and move *incredibly* fast. His character possessed the *amazing* ability to help people straighten out their hair problems— *The Human Conditioner.* Bertice and I felt that young Orenstein was a neurotically absorbed workaholic who didn't pay our Hannah enough attention. He claimed that he wasn't creating comics merely to entertain; his deeper purpose was to enlighten humanity by portraying *The Human Conditioner.* He was working an octurnal schedule, sleeping only one night in eight, turning night into week. Oney would ultimately break through years later with the *Normal Man* series, leading of course to the blockbuster Martin Scorcese film. Though Hannah still admires his work, Oney was not husband material. She wised up and moved on. We're not sure he noticed— in fact, he called a couple of weeks ago to ask if she knew where his green slippers were.

She took up with a young fellow from town who made oversized tennis rackets. He made her a beautifully matched pair of ornate turquoise and teal rackets she mounted in an X pattern on her bedroom wall, but it wasn't long before he became an ex as well. We never knew what the problem was.

After that, Hannah left the nest and moved in with a Doberman. There was conflict from the start. He wanted to go out all the time— she likes to stay in. She cut him some slack but he'd still snap at her. Eventually she forfeited her security deposit on the lease and moved back home. It didn't take a rocket scientist to see the guy was a dog.

Her next romantic interest was her finest boyfriend to date: Phil Ganderly, a centaur on the Milwaukee Bucks basketball team. We had high hopes for Hannah's "rebound" relationship: it takes a big man to be a big man in the NBA. His agent had had to convince the Bucks' brass to give Ganderly a shot coming out of Gonzaga: their general manager agreed that Phil had a lot of innate ability, but questioned his commitment to the game. A clause was added to his contract forbidding Ganderly from participating in horse racing. The haughty centaur thought the precaution ridiculous, as he explained to us over a glass of Shiraz: "Can you picture me galloping full out while pumping my arms on a racetrack? It's patently absurd."

Ganderly's game was necessarily a little different. Dribbling wasn't his strong suit, as he couldn't keep his torso consistently low enough to the ground without straining his legs: a pesky point guard could dart in and steal the ball from him fairly easily. This left him feeling like half a man out there, half hoarse from yelling for the ball. His strong suits were shot blocking, working the pick and roll, and cleaning up around the basket. Jump balls were no contest. We thrilled to Chuck Swirsky's game call cresting the pandemonium on the Bulls radio broadcasts: "And here's *another* tip-in by *GANderly*!!! Onions! Baby Onions! He IS *behooved*! He IS *behoooved*!!!" Fans grew to love the sight of him trotting back on defense after slam-dunking an alley-oop pass. He held his own against the great centers, Shaquille O'Neal, Tim Duncan; but if he'd eaten too heartily of oats and hay to get his energy up he'd often foul out before the end of the third quarter. "Well, I guess he's not the *only* one that's behooved to clean up around the basket. That is not a pretty sight down on the floor, Bill. We'll be back after this message."

Phil appeared on the Sports Illustrated cover, *Phil Ganderly— NBA CENTAUR*, posterizing Kobe Bryant, and was subsequently mobbed by press wherever he went. One night after a game he was cornered by a throng of crazed fans outside the stadium; "I am not an animal!" he cried. "I am a mythological being!" Rearing up on his hind legs to clear a space, he then leaped over the ravening fans and cantored majestically down the thoroughfare.

Phil would on occasion recount to us tales of his centaur forebears in Thessaly. Graciously updating our admittedly spotty Greek mythology, he told how Diameter became the Goddess of Girth; how Athena, goddess of wisdom, sprung fully blown from the head of Zeus; how Ares, god of war, sprung fully blown from the head of Athena. Although fallen from his former exalted position as King of the Gods on Mount Olympus, Zeus now greets and signs autographs for patrons of the Zeus Casino in Mount Cyprus. Aphrodite fell in love with the bubblegum character Bazooka Joe, arousing the envy of Phoebus Apollo, who turned Bazooka Joe into a peanut butter and mayonnaise sandwich. But before Apollo could consume him, the fleet-footed Artemis added anchovies, intending to permit Bazooka Joe to perish through a natural process of spoliation. Unbeknownst to the jealous rivals, Poseidon was soon to emerge from the depths of the wine-dark sea. Innocently sauntering by he espied and ate the sandwich before he realized what it was. For his trouble he was excoriated by proud Hera, and thus he sent Hermes to request Hephaestus to hammer out a beautiful diamond-and-ruby studded tiara for the Queen of the Gods, placating her wrath. Hephaestus in one of his blue funks did callously refuse, and while Hermes continued to plead Poseidon's case, Dionysus returned to earth to revive his orgiastic festivals. Poseidon said, "It was a lousy sandwich anyway," and neither Apollo nor Aphrodite have spoken to him since. Hephaestus at last relented, fashioning Hera a splendid tiara at his forge. Poseidon brought it to Hera, who declined the gift due to the inferior nature of the diamonds and rubies. "Well," said Poseidon, "I guess they can't all be gems." This, Ganderly inferred, accounts for contemporary geopolitical dialectics in Eurasia.

Hannah and Phil had a lovely time together— Ganderly became the centaur of her universe. She used to ride him around town on errands during the day, and judging from the huge racket coming through the bedroom wall, he'd return the favor at night. Sometimes, due to the incessant pounding, both of the rackets would come through.

Money was not an issue. In addition to his salary, Ganderly inked lucrative endorsement deals as a spokesman for Pegasus Horseshoes and Century 21.

But there were problems. Hannah would confide in her mother, who would of course pass the intimate details along to me. Hannah had cheerfully related that Phil was hung like a horse; but as time passed she grew indignant about some other physical aspects of the relationship the very private details of which I most certainly will not share here, having to do with the creature's smegma. Also she was afraid he'd roll over on her and kill her. It was difficult for us to envision her future as "Hannah Ganderly." Bertice was concerned about the possibility of our grandchildren living out their lives as quarter horses. Things became untenable. Through no fault of his own, the centaur had become the elephant in the living room.

I had a father-daughter discussion with Hannah, quoting of course from Hamlet:

> "And that in way of caution— I must tell you,
> You do not understand yourself so clearly
> As it behooves my daughter and your honor.
> What is between you? Give me up the truth."

"Mind your own business, Dad."

"It is my business. I'm the one who has to keep plastering the wall."

We wanted to return to our normal, quiet suburban life. And there's only one way to stop a dominating NBA centaur: put a body on him. I went and got a corpse from the basement freezer early one morning, hauled it furtively into Hannah's bedroom and hoisted it up onto the snoring Ganderly.

Phil threw it off, jumped through the patio door screen and bounded up over the wall, galloping swiftly back to the more predictable sanctuary of pure archetype.

There was of course a repair expense for the screen, but we felt it was a small price to pay. And during the summer months, Hannah found she was just as happy with the frozen corpse.

Like kayaks on the high seas, like the continents through millennia, like loosely packed snowmen, Bertice and I drifted apart.

Is there a sex witholding tax?

I for my part had sublimated my yearnings into obsessiveness with the Star Wars movies and video games. One day Bertice came in and threw my joystick across the room. "May divorce be with you," she said through clenched teeth, and walked out. "That's a lousy pun," I called after her. "This is how you're ending a marriage?"

The ensuing depression was broodle.

I tried to hang myself but couldn't get the noose working and decided it was knot to be.

I called my friend Bannerman for support. He told me to live each day as if it were to be my last. So I lay in bed all day moaning.

This was the beginning of a time of spiritual searching for me— a voyage of self-discovery.

A therapist helped me to access and integrate my life story. She encouraged me to get out and try new things.

My life drawing class, employing Alzheimer's victims, opened up a whole nude dementia.

I struggled earnestly with self-help and co-dependency books. The books' flow of entertaining yet instructive prose was continually interrupted by sidebar quotes from eminent individuals such as Baba Ram Dass, Mother Theresa and Aristotle. I didn't know whether to stop reading the text when I turned the page and read the quotes, or read all the quotes in the book first, or read them when I was finished, or read them as I got up to them, losing track of the narrative. There were workshop questions at the ends of the chapters, stressing the points repeated thrice each during the chapter.

The co-dependency book typically opens with a third person scene describing an intransigent problem between two of the author's former clients— let's call them John and Cindy. John, an electrical contractor, comes home from work and finds Cindy, a software troubleshooter, working at her computer station, snacking on fruit roll-ups and almonds, and no other food in the house. "*Bitch!*" John shouts angrily, "I been loving you since *DAY ONE* and I ain't got no dinner!" Cindy, rather than understand that John grew up in a working class family where the mother's job was to always have dinner ready, withdraws to her room in a huff. The couple hasn't had sex in three months. Should they get a divorce? The couple comes to the therapist/author, learn active listening techniques and then— after a period where they agree to work at it, letting go of shame-driven patterns and undergoing a trial-and-error period of establishing boundaries— the relationship, though no longer a honeymoon, is transformed into one of trust and mutual support.

Now, when John comes home and shouts, "*Bitch*, where the hell's my stinkin' *DINNER*," Cindy says, "You had me at 'bitch,' John. You had me at 'bitch,'" and the couple off go to a time-share bungalow for the weekend.

The therapist/author is pictured on the back, fit, tanned and bursting with wellness, grinning like a mandrill on his or her backlit designer patio in California.

The self-help book would lift my spirits for two or three weeks, but I would soon sink back into paroxysms of self-loathing and moral lassitude. Then I would feel guilty, and purchase another self-help book.

My therapist suggested I take the once-a-week chewable supplement for the seasonally affected: Chews D.

I affixed wise 'n' witty affirmations to the refrigerator:

Evolve, already.

Today is the third day of the rest of your life.

Don't sweat the holocaust. And, it's *all* holocaust.

I didn't have much luck taking it "a day at a time," but found that twenty-seven hour increments worked best for me.

I went through a costly past life regression. I was hoping to have been Julius Caesar, or Alexander the Great, or even Mary, Queen of Scots. It happened that in the third century BC, I was a man in what is now Kazakhstan, who went on errands.

A hypnotherapist took me on a spirit quest to find my totem animal. One imagines the eagle, the bear, the tiger, the snake, sensing liberating spiritual potentialities in all of these energies. But my totem animal turned out to be an anteater.

There was a new age meditation storefront a couple blocks down on the corner. I signed up for a five-week, four-hour mythopoetic spirituality workshop.

The third week in, my meditation guru got so flustered and frustrated with my inveterate twitching and tapping on the linoleum that he lost his temper with me. "Live in the now, punk," he hissed furiously and fled the room, tripping on his robe and taking a header into the middle of a Tai Chi class in progress in the adjoining studio.

Seeking a religion that wears well, I went to a Bootist temple.

We had to elect our church officials. One candidate was a guy who listened to taped meditations all the time on his headset— a natural for the office of Ombudsman.

Then I joined the Culinary Church, where a man can worship as he chews.

Being born again is different for different people.

Followers of Christ sat in the Christian section; followers of Caesar in the Caesarean section.

Where the followers of Christ would partake of the bread and wine, followers of Caesar would have the salad.

The Christians were at peace with the Caesareans. Their real conflict was with the vegetarians.

The place had started as a Methodist Church. Their good minister had had the idea to have food prepared to go with various passages of scripture; the generations of the bread, Ruth amid the alien corn, passages relating to anise, cinnamon, grapes and so forth. Some of the church members took the ball and ran with it, preparing more and more elaborate meals based on the next week's sermon's tangential food reference.

More and more people started coming to church, and they began to hire professional chefs. By the end of their third year, they had a general chef, a French chef, and a vegan chef, alternating every third week. The minister quoted from *Matthew 23:23*:

"Woe unto you, scribes and Pharisees, hypocrites! for ye pay tithe of mint and anise and cumin, and have omitted the weightier matters of the law, judgment, mercy, and faith: these ought ye to have done, and not to leave the other undone."— and resigned his position.

Folks did not make an unseemly display of their relief, but the general feeling was jeez, what a stick-in-the-mud that guy was!

The new minister, a portly gent, had bought into the new program. "Thankful for the first bloom in the garden, lettuce spray," he opened, beaming to huge applause. Then, "This is a day the Lord has made. Let's eat!"

We all lined up to meet him. "It's Andrew Calhoun," I said, and offered my hand. "Good to know you Andy," he cooed, squeezing my hand affirmingly and leaning in to massage my elbow. "Calhoun! (slapping my shoulder) Good name, good name."

From then on there were brief weekly sermons and a time for the congregation to share from their hearts. Often members would make prayer requests for distant cousins who would be attempting soufflés that week.

The church brought in celebrities eager to promote their products; George Foreman came to talk about his faith, and demonstrated his grill. He really had nice teeth.

The Hall of Fame relief pitcher Rich Gossage stopped in to promote his new line of breakfast meats: Goose Gossage's Sausages, as well as Goose Gossage's Reduced Fat Sausages.

"That's a mouthful!" punned the new minister.

Jessye Williams shared stories from her wonderful book, Herbal Lore Galore. There were lots of useful tips. She told us that chamomile repels insects and promotes healing. I had to ask myself— am I an insect? Marjoram, used as a floor wash, will dispel negativity and promote love and happiness. I felt a tinge of guilt suspecting that any herb, used as a floor wash, will perform this function.

Franchises came to do demos: A local "Fruit 'n' Fish" smoothie company came and prepared samples of their orange orange roughie smoothie.

Every third week Chef Thibault created a new recipe. First time I went it was root vegetables with saffron and parsley, boiled in Perrier. A Soup Perrier dish, supplemented by a ratatouille with eggplant, ratatats and tomatoes. His "Revelations" of flaming flan in the lake of blood (an intense cherry reduction) brought the house down.

The second week Chef Scott (his first name) prepared a Mulligatawny, timed to be ready to be removed from the heat at the exact same time as the Chicken Almond Ding. That Sunday's presentation from the peppy, fast-talking rep for a pancake mix called "Scratch" went over big. Chef Scott was in on this, and when he got compliments on his berried-in-custard dessert crepe, said, "Don't give me the credit— I made it from 'Scratch!'"

The third week I brought a couple of vegetarian friends along. Our vegan chef Skye (her only name) was scheduled to make a curry, but opted to make a turmeric instead. There was a light dessert of helium dumplings. And we learned that all vegetables are really fruits. We all had the dumplings, but when we got back in the car I was the only one having a problem. I didn't think I'd be solo on gas.

Our new minister had requested that Chef Thibault purchase wild caught salmon to broil and serve with *crème fraîche* the following week. "I'm not that kind of a chef," he said, "you don't get *fraîche* with me." He delivered instead a basal ganglia tortellini with shiitake mushrooms and wild rice. His meal was finished with flourless chocolate cake— a no-grainer.

A burgundy pant-suited rep demoed a spring-driven wind-up can opener that would hump its way around a tuna can in eight seconds. "And that's it! So as you can see, our automatic can opener... is a real eye opener!"

"You're kind of an eye-opener yourself, sugar!" leered the new minister before assuming his solemnity aspect for the week's reading in *Corinthians*.

Chef Scott followed up with a trio of bone-in ham, Tuscan chicken and tusk-in boar, with creamed spinach. He explained that protein and carbohydrates are essential elements in the cuisine of the Friuli-Venezia Giulia Region of Italy. He garnered mixed reviews with a rather dry marzipan cake served on opalescent plates the size of garbage can lids with pomegranate/acai berry syrup drizzled around them.

Chef Skye trumped him a week later, partnering spice marinades with various beans; creating a garlic saffron lima, a nutmeg coriander black bean, and currying fava. The appetizer was pumpkin/zucchini/cabbage soup. "The reason I eat all these pureed soups is, it gives me that certain vegetable magnetism," she winked. She would try to convert the church omnivores to veganism with pithy lectures delivered with a breezy, seemingly effortless sensuality, and animal slaughterhouse abuse videos shown during the meal.

This did not pass without objection. And by the same token, some felt the church had taken the communion ceremony too far. The body and the blood were now accompanied by the intestines (spaghetti), the eyeballs (melon balls), and the hair (shaved Belgian dark chocolate with hazelnuts).

Church membership divided slowly but surely into three camps. There were only a few of us who came for all the chefs. And so it was decided that we would have a picnic at Lake Illini Lake, an hour and twenty minutes Northwest of the city, on the first Saturday in May, in order to reaffirm our sense of community. Each chef would prepare a main dish, but we were all invited to contribute our humble offerings to the potluck.

I decided to make a cob salad. I took several cobs from ears of corn I had eaten over the previous months, and put them through a food processor, then stirred in a few cans of baby corn. Following up on a tip from the chefs, I added salt and pepper to taste; if you add them to not taste there's no point in adding them at all.

Art Landry brought five boxes of 100 tea bags each. That's Salada tea.

Everybody was having a great time. The new minister was there in a festive Hawaiian shirt and Bermuda shorts, presiding assuredly over the flock, bestowing nicknames with a wink upon any not already blessed with one. Kids were running around, little boys shrieking in perpetual crescendo. When I get sentimental about the old din days, I think of those boys. The younger girls were making a lentils garland, and a split peas hoop. Other girls were off snooping around trees, indulging in various age-appropriate brands of vicious gossip.

Chef Scott chain-smoked, pacing, waiting for a delivery. I introduced myself, and told him how much I'd loved his Ding, and we chatted a bit. "This isn't all that I do," he said with a dismissive wave of the hand, "I also trade on the financial markets." I didn't know much about money management, so I used one of my stock phrases— "Buy low, sell high," I said. He also was an investor in vestments: there were plans for a chain of stores for clothing the clergy called "Robe Us."

I asked him if I could pick his brain about mutual funds. "I hate it when someone tells me they want to pick my brain," he said irritably. "I visualize one of those silver nut picks we used to dig out walnuts with." Then, "Delivery!" he called joyously as a poultry truck rolled in over the grass. When I turned to look he stubbed his cigarette out in my butt crack. I regretted playing up to him about the Ding— undercooked chicken with overcooked peas, stale slivered almonds and a lousy can of cream of mushroom soup.

Chef Thibault's preparation was done ahead of time; he had brought three coolers full of *Salade Niçoise*, and was relaxing, sharing a cigar with his lover Philippe, a renowned Olympic fencer from Alsace-Lorraine. We struck up a conversation. Of course I asked them if they were interested in baseball. "I'm a big fan a major league *bouillabaisse!*" said the balding Philippe, in halting English. "You mean major league baseball?" "No— minor league *bouillabaisse!*" They found this hilarious. To them I think it was an entendre of some kind. Philippe scowled at the plenitude of trays of Lime Jell-O slathered in whipped cream. "I sheet on it!"— he said, over and over. It was one of six or eight English sentences he had mastered. Becky Landry had brought a large fruit salad with honey cinnamon dressing. We were afraid the fruit salad would be covered with flies by the time dinner was served, but fortunately Philippe was eager to demonstrate his fencing skills, on point to fend them off with his aluminum foil.

He kept going on and on about the Jell-O. Finally I took him aside and told him I thought his remarks were slightly off-pudding.

Blender drinks are a mixed blessing. Someone thought some frozen limas would bean ice in a margarita.

I'd brought my guitar, a way of making friends as I am an otherwise shy person, and sang "Crawdad Song," and "Big Yam Taters in the Sandy Land." The new minister said, "Hey, *you've* got some talent. But you don't have to only sing about *food*, folksinger guy." Then he said,

"What kind of guitar is that?"

The new minister disappeared at some point during our water volleyball game. Due to the ensuing rhubarb, nobody realized he was gone until his body drifted in a few days later.

Chef Scott had decided to push it with the vegans, bringing in several chickens and a turkey to slaughter and roast on the spot. There was a tussle, during which most of the chickens escaped to an adjoining cornfield. The vegans were joined in *entente cordiale* by Chef Thibault and Philippe (who were simply offended by Chef Scott's cooking) in pounding him to a bloody pulp. More dishes were thrown than eaten. It's safe to say that things ended badly for the Culinary Church.

But not for me. There was an attractive young widow there, smelling and looking good, I'll tell you, cloved in a tight saffron dress with fenugreek scarf and cardamom sweater. Though only a recent churchgoer, I took seriously the injunction to care for the widow's endorphins. I packed up the remainder of the cob salad and asked her to walk up around the lake with me. She was a heavy-lidded woman with neck problems. I suggested she try wearing a lighter lid. And that seemed to do the trick.

We wondered how people can get so fanatical about their food intake that they can only hang out with other people who share their particular culinary inclinations. We decided to avoid the diet tribes. We agreed that the new minister was a jackass, and that the old minister was a jackass, and that the chefs and deacons and everyone in the church but us were basically jackasses and we didn't care for their noisy children, either.

She, like myself, was on a spiritual search.

We debated the big questions:

Is the glass half empty, or does it not even exist at all, except in our imaginations?

Is the glass half full, or does it not even exist at all, except in our imaginations?

What if the glass is entirely full?

Following our initial flurry of hormone-induced agreeability, we were a contentious couple. We weren't sure if we were in love with each other, or in love with love, or in love with arguing, because we spent so much time arguing about whether or not we were actually arguing.

I mentioned I wasn't crazy about Yosemite National Park.

"Yo! Are you anti-semitic?"

"I'm half Jewish."

"Those are the worst."

"Did I ask you?"

"Am I telling you?"

"Are you arguing with me?"

"I'm not arguing."

Like competitive shoppers in a department store, issues would escalate. We struggled to find common ground.

We went to the museum, which was usually packed but it was dead that day. We enjoyed the Old Masters room, but felt that they could have used more Titians.

After our few gluttonous weeks in the foodie church, we made a pact to lose weight, or diet trying.

We went on the Smidgen Diet.

Smidgen Diet

DAY ONE:

Breakfast:

1/3 cup oatmeal

1/6 of a poached egg

3/8 of a slice of whole wheat toast with 1/6 of an ounce of olive oil on it (optional)

an 11-ounce glass of water

Lunch:

1/3 cup oatmeal

1/4 cup of cottage cheese

1/2 grapefruit

sloppy joe

10 ounces of decaffeinated coffee or peppermint tea

Dinner:

1/8 of a medium size chicken breast

two stalks of asparagus

a 14-ounce glass of water

DAY TWO

Breakfast:

3 goat kidneys, grilled

juice made from beets, kohlrabi and dinosaur kale

Lunch:

3 ounce (before cooking) hamburger with 1/4 tsp mustard (optional) wrapped in iceberg lettuce

two tomato slices

3/8 cup of cottage cheese

Dinner:

2/9 cup of cottage cheese

steamed parsnips.

pencil shavings

7 ounces of 1% milk

DAY THREE

Breakfast:

one slice of toast

stewed peach

decaf coffee

Lunch:

2 marinated prunes

1/5 cup of cottage cheese

12 oz 1% milk *or* 9 oz decaf coffee *or* 11 oz chamomile tea

Dinner:

4oz turkey breast

1/3 cup grilled zucchini

panty hose

bran muffin

8 oz water with juice of 1/3 lemon

Once a month we'd blow the diet and go for dinner at Campy's. The place had huge portions— their mini-burgers were the size of burgers.

We went to the U. U. Church, reputed to be open, tolerant and diverse. They cater to people who enjoy using church in a utilitarian way. There we encountered some of the most diverse people we ever met. After the first half came the "passing of the U's," during which we were induced to introduce ourselves. The first time we went we sat next to a woman who looked like Lieutenant Uhura. She had nappy hair, and her foot kept falling asleep as well. "Are you Ugandan?" we asked her. Indeed she was, and she in turn introduced us to her partner Eunice, from the former Soviet Union; "Are you Ukrainian?" we asked her, and indeed she was, a Ukrainian urologist who introduced us to Uri, a usurer; "Are you from Uruguay?" we asked him, and indeed he was; "Are you from Uruguay too?" asked Hugh, his partner; and so it went.

Those in grief and those who wished to support them were encouraged to ululate lugubriously during the service intermission. An Ubi masseuse from Singapore demonstrated laying-on-of-hands techniques involved in universal healing energy. After that we made a ritual of saying "Ubian touch" when someone had to leave early. The congregation was universally delighted and ultimately moved by a visit from Bishop Tutu. I was asked to sing U. Utah Phillips' "All Used Up" for this occasion. We were exhorted to celebrate Diversity, along with Christmas and Easter, but it wasn't clear which day it fell on, or what we were supposed to do on Diversity. It goes to show you you never can tell about the U. U. The widow and I made an unusually unanimous decision to move on.

We went to a Baptist church. We loved the fervent hymn-singing, but they had a minister who thought it was instructive to baptize converts by holding them under water for two to three minutes, gaping mawkishly at the congregation, until he finally let them up gasping for air and spluttering.

I was able to sleep through the stultifying Old Testament readings, but the widow had trouble sleeping in church, due to inpsalmnia.

She had a less serious problem than her psalmnambulent brother.

Outside of church we discussed various outlooks on afterlife and immortality of the soul. She wanted to discuss Hell again, but I said, "Look, let's not go there."

She insisted I should return to my roots, and see a Jewish rabbi. "Look," I snapped at her, "I'm perfectly comfortable with my Baptist rabbi." Which was true. I wasn't planning to be baptized anyway. At last, she prevailed.

We went to a synagogue where we had trouble following the complexities of what the rabbi was saying through his thick accent. To illustrate, the venerable scholar made a visible exegesis by tipping a crucifix sideways.

I told him I was looking for myself. "Oy," he said, "Who's doing the looking?"

At last I felt that my control issues were under control.

I improved my social climbing skills with the aid of a nutritional supplement called Bounder-ease. Even my therapist was impressed. She asked me if I had anything else I wanted to work on. I said I felt pretty good about things, but it bothered me that I kept feeling compelled to murder people. She said she wouldn't feel comfortable with that either. She suggested that that was an issue I wasn't quite ready to really deal with at this point in my life story. She questioned whether I'd ever, as an artist, be truly comfortable with being comfortable. We agreed that I'd healed from the divorce, and it was time to suspend the therapy. I brought my guitar to the last session, and played her some of my most intense and revealing songs. In the back of my mind, I felt that we had already done the hard work of getting to know and trust each other. She seemed accepting of all that I was, and I thought that maybe in a few months, we could spend some time together as friends and see what might develop. She already knew the most intimate details of my life and psyche, of course, but I had never before shared my *art*. "Pretty!" she said.

"What kind of guitar is that?"

A good therapist is hard to find. And indeed she never was.

The widow and I got into terrific shape, with our running arguments, and that next summer we decided to run a marathon, arguing all the way to the shoe store to shop for running shoes. I got a shoe called the Nike Go-Strider, which claimed that it would do my running for me. She got the Adidas Running Commentary, which she claimed was the superior shoe. We placed third together in the Chicago marathon, crossing the line at the same moment in a show of mutual determination and harmony. I had held back to let her cross with me, but she claimed to have done the same.

Shortly thereafter, I dumped the widow and moved on.

"It's not ye," I said, "it's mou."

She said she'd been planning to break up with me but at least had had the decency to wait until after the next trip to Campy's.

If I'd known I was going to write this book all these years later, I'd have asked her what her name was.

Well, we had a good run.

Coming down from the rebound relationship, I was looking for a woman with a big heart, small intestines, and a cleft chin.

A few months later I was coming out of the corner 7-Eleven with a bag holding a pint of Cherry Sherbet, a couple bananas and a roll of toilet tissue. She was leaning against the wall, cooling off in style with an Artisan Slurpee. The pooper-scooper law was recently in effect, and she was out with her basset hound, then taking a steaming dump on the sidewalk. She looked at me with embarrassment and said she'd left the house without a plastic bag. Was she afraid I'd call the police, or just think less of her? I reached into my bag and gallantly brandished the Scott tissue roll. "Dude! Did you just pull that out of your ass?"

She liked dumb-looking guys, she told me later, and thought I was the anderthal's knees.

We toddled over to the local hipster cafe, the North Angst, and she ordered the bottomless cup of Mobius drip coffee.

When we parted at her apartment building, I blew a kiss. Maybe I was just too self-conscious or something.

Our next date went better. We thrilled to Mel Gibson shouting "You cannae tak oor freedom!!!" in Brayfart.

Annie had been divorced for two years, and had run out of settlement money. She'd tried going back to school, majoring in bio with a minor in Ed. But she failed the bio and dropped Ed shortly thereafter.

She said she'd marry again or else flip burgers if she could find an eligible spatula.

We had a beautiful ceremony.

"Take a low doff, Annie," said the minister. So she removed her hat and bowed down to the level of her knee.

I ravished her in her wedding dress the moment we got to the hotel; it was to be a lifetime commitment, and I wanted to gain her trussed.

But I couldn't get pasta spaghetti strap. You never sausage a mess.

We enjoyed following the Cubs. At that time the team was moving farther and farther to the right politically, as they continued to sign Dominican Republicans.

We knew they were in for a long year when the closer blew the opener.

That summer they rocked the baseball world by signing their scoreboard operator to play first base. Their general manager said he was the only guy in the outfield who had been able to put up numbers consistently during April and May.

The man was a five-tool ballplayer. His pants fit like a glove.

The Cubs' problem was with their middle relief pitching. Our hearts would sink as their hapless manager trudged to the mound to signal for a right-hander named Todd or Wayne. New to the team each year, these journeymen would enter during the interminable mid-game to surrender three to five runs apiece over their inning and a thirds.

I recall a game the Cubbies were leading 4-0 in the fourth inning, when manager Bud Franklin sent up a batter to hit for the pitcher. By the last of the eighth, two Waynes and a Todd had yielded thirteen runs. The Cubs lost 14-5. After the game in the interview room, Franklin was asked by perplexed and/or furious reporters to explain this curious decision. "Well, there are more important things in life than baseball. And one of those things is family." That sort of put the jackals at bay. "That's true," acknowledged the Sun-Times beat reporter, "But that doesn't explain the decision. Is there an injury situation?" "Nah. Look, my cousin owns a bowling alley over on Roscoe. He was short three pins due to employee theft, with the supply shop closed and the Sunday afternoon leagues coming in at 4 p.m. So I sent O'Brien up there, and he saved the day with a pin shit triple."

Annie made some side income writing soft porn articles for magazines. She got a special commission to write a sex manual based on the Kama Sutra. This began to take up all of her time, and I must admit, I felt a bit neglected. So, taking the advice of a new Andy Goodman self-help book on creative relationship, *Breaking the Patterns that Bind Us*, rather than express my selfish resentment I went in and began rubbing her shoulders and tenderly kissing the back of the neck. "Jesus," she said, "Can't you see I'm writing a fucking book?"

I suspected Annie was faking orgasms, because it seemed like she was always ovary acting.

We never seemed to have any money. Annie had a secret passion.

Gambling addiction? You bet. She was playing roulette with our finances.

In an effort to patch things up, I gave her a brooch with two "o"s in it. But the relationship descended into bitter acronymy.

And we got a divorce, LOL.

I didn't come out of it too badly, because I was able to prove that Annie had posed for pin-up shots during the marriage, in violation of our pinuptual agreement.

After a period of years, the reason for the second divorce became clear to me. My penis was too large, and all of my wife's acting out was just to hide the fact that she wasn't comfortable with it. So she used a technique called *misdirection.*

I've since compensated for the technique by using Viagra.

I still think about filing for divorce. But they won't let you do that unless you're currently married. Is that discrimination?

When times get rough I still lean on my ex, Bertice.

My dad had been a successful actor, but in his fifties he went into theatre pedagogy; and while some found him a bit pompous— a bit of a pedant perhaps— he did produce several major stars from the forge of his workshop, "Scientific Method Acting." The slogan was "Think Globally— Act Professionally." As he aged he lost none of his patented vigor but had trouble following the course of the plays due to occasional memory lapses and failing hearing and vision. So we bought him a scene guide dog.

At the last, he lent his name to a local production of Arsenic and Old Lace, returning to live theatre in what would be remembered as his most convincing performance, perishing as if on cue, of an aneurysm. While he had generated mixed feelings in the community, he was respected for living according to his lights and, in the end, didactic.

My mother is still with us. Well, at the time of this writing. She may well be dead by the time you read this.

Once, I dreamed of a middle class life. But the dream is slipping away, and being replaced by one in which I am digging up bright pink turnips with a sort of verdigris sheen in Herbert Hoover's garden, which is atop the Empire State Building at first, and then creating clay hand imprints with my fourth-grade teacher who now looks like Kate Jackson and then turns into a panda in Jackson, Tennessee.

THE MEM WARS OF ANDREW CALHOUN TRILOGY
PART 3: LIFE *TODAY*

It does behoove the cattle producer to understand the inheritance of color, enabling him to predict with some accuracy the color pattern of his calf crop and know how to change it.

— B.C. ALLISON,
Animal Husbandry Newsletter, 1996.

I have come to accept that I'm nearly as old as I am.

Sure, I'll admit to some denial. I just question whether it's truly massive.

I haven't given up on my dream of becoming a household word. So I'm changing my name to Toaster.

Last night I dreamed I woke up, and when I awoke I found it was a dream come true.

Things I used to think of as preposterous are now postposterous.

You probably won't believe this, but there was a leviathan in the kitchen when I went down for breakfast. A *leviathan*! What do you do? You can't *know,* ahead of time, how you'll actually behave in a situation. "Get out! Get out!" I screamed, and whacked it a few times with a broom. Apparently it got the message, because it isn't there now.

Today I threw a couple stoats in the pot for breakfast. Kind of a strong flavor, so I tempered it by adding an eel. I took it outside and sat out on the front porridge swing, eating eel-cut stoats.

The laundry was getting to be a crisis, so I took it to the detergency room.

Home is where the yard is.

Lawn forcement came by last week and told us to mulch our leaves.

We don't mind coyotes prowling the neighborhood, as long as they share our values.

Neighbor's hound left a lovely mess by the mailbox. That's pretty mutt shit for today.

I set up a workstation with a computer and fax capabilities in the neighbors' backyard. When they asked why, I said "So your dog will stop doing his business over here."

Someone left a big pile of grist on the front porch. So I'm writing about it.

Got a couple cans of driveway sealer laid away in the shed. Planning for my retarment.

Last night I noticed the flue to the fireplace had been left open, and heat would be escaping, so I went to close it up. Then I saw there was this huge insect jammed in it, and it was straining with all six of its remarkably strong arm-thingys to keep it open. I hadn't expected to spend the entire evening fighting a flue bug.

There are men working on the place. It's a hexagonal house, and all week they've been nailing up aluminum. It's six-siding work.

Today they're cutting wood for window trim in the dining room, and putting a new edition on the house. The New Palgrave Dictionary of Economics is replacing one of the loose shingles.

They suggested I should get a new skeptic tank, but I said I wasn't convinced that that would solve the problem.

They said it would have been easier to fix the roof if I hadn't kept tarping on it.

They did repair the iron rail by the front porch. Weld done.

They are professionals, and will not point at my sticking-up hair and laugh when I stumble down for coffee. Construction people are preferable to friends on this account. But you have to pay them. I could pay friends not to laugh. But that might just make them laugh more.

Small projects around the place, I do myself. For example, the dowels holding this chair I'm sitting on together were getting a little loose, but fortunately Ace hardware was offering free dowel nodes.

Scrutinizing tiny screws is excruciating.

I tried to unclog the drain with the snake, but it didn't work. I guess there was a reptile dysfunction.

I pulled the old bicycle out of the shed, oiled it up and pumped up the tires. Hadn't ridden in years, but when I got up on it, it was like riding a bike. Took it down to the bike shop for a tune-up, but they told me it needed to be re-tired.

While I was walking downtown, a guy took out a gun and shot at me, but I jumped out of the way. I think I may have dodged a bullet there.

Then on the way home a guy threw a chicken out of a car, but again I jumped out of the way. I think I may have dodged a pullet there.

While buzzing around thrift stores today, I picked up a barely used paternity suit at the resale shop over in Wheaton.

I kept getting raw sewage from the blimp falling on the house and yard. So I wrote a dirigible john letter.

My health club was recently sold to a Christian organization. First all the entrance clerks started saying "Have a blessed workout." Then this morning an employee approached me at the treadmill and asked if I was ready to accept Jesus as my personal trainer.

I'm nursing a bad hamstring. So far it won't take any milk, though.

I took an abbreviated sauna, as several guys got into a heated discussion.

I'm presenting a "bi-regional touring workshop" in January, in Hawaii. If someone will fly me there.

I'm currently working on the sordid tale of *Crypt Dick,* which, when I get the plot fleshed out, will be either a vampire novel or a biography of Dick Cheney.

I'm still inspired to write a song occasionally. From new pop lyric, "You Are the Light":

"You are the light, that shines in shining things

You are the anti-perspirant beneath my wings."

———

Tonight I went over to the Two-Way Street Coffeehouse in Downers Grove to hear Muriel Anderson's CD-release concert in the big room. She played O'Carolan tunes, notes flowing in precise cascades; old-time flat-picking barnburners; a scintillating Flamenco piece; Chet Atkins swing guitar. She played a remarkable instrument; a guitar with an additional harp-looking section added on, with extra bass strings.

I went up and waited my turn to say hello and have my CD signed. I intended to comment on the Flamenco; to mention that a mutual friend had said to say hey; to ask how she'd been. I didn't do any of those things. Instead I asked:

"What kind of guitar is that?"

I'm not convinced by my autopsy results; going in tomorrow for a second opinion.

Then I was bestowed my wings, though through some odd chance I was only given one. "Surely there must be some mistake," said I. "Can I get a second pinion?"

A voice came down, saying only, "You are behooved to wear one wing." And indeed, I had the lower half and hooves of a cow. I guess I look pretty ridiculous.

One wing, with which to spiral on up to the pearly gates. Ungainly, and exhausting, and the news isn't good. Saint Peter said, "Look, Cow-hoon. You murdered seventy-eight people, and sang 'Kum Ba Yah.' On balance, you're not gettin' in here."

"Well I'll be damned."

"Nice one, Cow-hoon. Are you trying to be funny?"

THE MEM WARS OF ANDREW CALHOUN TRILOGY
EPILOGUE

*And it behoveth also, that the place that men have pissed in
be hallowed again, and else dare no man enter therein.*

— SIR JOHN MANDEVILLE

A fter all the *sturm und drang,* it's really not much of a change. When I got here, Satan approached with his horns, goat hooves and pitchfork, the infernal knob of his engorged member glistening in the firelight.

"Play 'The Scotsman'", he commanded.

"Sorry, I don't know that one."

"You don't fucking know *'The Scotsman?'* I can't believe they let you in here. Hey, don't let the gates hit you in the ass on the way out."

Even a damned right-wing cow has to draw the line somewhere.

If you need a ghostwriter, please contact my agent.

— Andy Goodman

Life is not about the destination.

It's about the Guernsey.